Working On A
Dream

A Year on the Road with Waterford Footballers

Damian Lawlor

MENTOR
BOOKS

First published in 2009 by
Mentor Books Ltd.,
43 Furze Road
Sandyford Industrial Estate
Dublin 18
Republic of Ireland

Tel: +353 1 295 2112/2   Fax: +353 1 295 2114
e-mail: admin@mentorbooks.ie
www.mentorbooks.ie

A catalogue record for this book is available from the British Library

ISBN: 978-1-906623-40-1

Cover: Kathryn O'Sullivan
Typesetting and layout: Kathryn O'Sullivan
Editor: Treasa O'Mahony

Printed in Ireland by ColourBooks Ltd

Acknowledgements

The publishers would like to thank Sportsfile for permission to reproduce
images.

Contents

Foreword

I've scarcely enjoyed a year as much as this one.

Thanks to Jackson for opening the doors to his set-up and shoving me right in. It's unbelievable, not even once did he ask to see sample chapters of this book or seek to put the clampers on me. He was wide open and completely put his trust in me. He knew that I wasn't tagging the team just to poke fun at his lads and he was happy enough with that. For all his co-operation, friendship, enthusiasm and encouragement, I offer a thousand thanks. For the bad jokes and asking me to give a pep talk at half-time in Waterford's crucial league game against Sligo, not so much thanks! Jackson kept this show on the road for the past five years and everyone responds to him. It's easy to see why.

To his backroom team, Mick, Paul, Tom and Ger, I appreciate every bit of help you gave. It was a pleasure stalking you for the year.

Thanks to the players, otherwise known as Jackson's 'warriors'. I really couldn't have any more admiration for you. Keep knocking on the door and the day will soon come when you wave goodbye to Division 4. Your perspective, commitment and enthusiasm for what many would consider a lost cause is nothing short of inspirational. Respect to every one of you and thanks for the chats, interviews, phone calls and texts. I can't ever repay you for such a warm welcome into the set-up. Thanks for sharing your story.

To my lovely wife, Ruth, whom I married in August 2009, thanks for your patience and understanding. You pushed me all the way on this project and I'm a lucky man to have you by my side. I spent the year on the byroads of Ireland, trying to fit everything in and your encouragement shortened the journey. Asking you to marry me was one of my better moves!

To my publisher Danny McCarthy at Mentor Books, thanks for taking a punt on this project at a time when big-name blockbuster autobiographies are all the rage, I am forever grateful. He called it straight all year long and his constructive criticism kept me on the straight and narrow. To Treasa, my editor, who kept me focused and moulded this thing into shape, a thousand thanks. You were a reassuring, calm presence from start to finish.

Thanks also to my good friend Richie Gallagher whose advice and constructive criticism were invaluable to me. Richie has a way with words that very few have and his help was greatly appreciated as always.

Damien Eagers and Michael Kiely supplied the photographs, while Dave O'Leary and Ciaran Farren gave me lots of help with the design.

As always, my friends from the media world were there. Jackie Cahill, Christy O'Connor, Finbarr McCarthy, Kieran Shannon, Cian Murphy, Paul Collins, Brian Carthy and Brendan Fanning all offered huge support and plenty of ideas along the way. Real good men. Thanks also to John Greene in the *Sunday Independent* for his understanding during the year. I couldn't let the opportunity pass without mentioning my great friend Liam Dunne. We wrote *I Crossed the Line* together and I missed his company on this project.

Finally, to my family, especially my parents John and Mary, I look back on my childhood and all I have are happy memories. That's down to you both.

Damian Lawlor, September 2009

I'd like to dedicate this book to the memory
of my great friend
Carol Seymour, Ballycommon, Nenagh
who passed away on
8 October 2008.

You are sorely missed but you will never be forgotten.
May you rest in peace, Carol.

Cast of characters

Waterford Senior Football Team:

John 'Jackson' Kiely – Waterford Senior Football Manager

Mick O'Loughlin – Physical Trainer and Coordinator

Stephen 'Budgie' Cunningham – Veteran of 15 seasons

Paul McLoughlin – Skills Coach, former Kildare footballer

Paul Ogle (Ogie) – Defender and GPA representative

Mick Ahearne (Mickah) – Long-serving midfielder

Tom Wall – Goalkeeper

Ger Power – Wing-forward

Maurice and Thomas O'Gorman – Defenders

Gary Hurney – Waterford hurling and football dual star

Jason Ryan – Current Wexford football manager and former Waterford
    stalwart

Liam Lawlor – Scottish-based student

Tom Condon & Ger Power – Selectors

Liam Ó Líonáin – Top scorer

Brian Wall – Freetaker

Eddie Rockett, Tony Grey, Shane Briggs and John Phelan – Defenders

Cillian O'Keeffe and Seán O'Hare – Students

Stephen Prendergast and John Hayden – Defenders

Mel Shanley – Weights coach

Cian O'Connor – Physiotherapist

Dave Kenneally – Stamina coach

Johnny Grace – Masseur

Michael Scanlon – First Aid

Prologue

4 July 2009, Páirc Tailteann, Navan

ONE by one they trudge to the showers, barely uttering a word, the stillness of the dank dressing-room air punctuated only by the thud of water bottles hitting the floor and the clattering of studs on the corridor outside.

The evening has assumed the texture of one of those frustrating dreams, where you prepare for something for so long and then you don't turn up. It's just another weekend in the life of a Waterford footballer.

Outside in the All-Ireland qualifiers, the team has just been handed a lesson by Meath. It was game over after 20 minutes or thereabouts and so the curtain fell on the show for another six months. Defeat has long been a staple diet for Waterford footballers but they know there's some bit of sustenance to be found in the dressing room. Sure, the sores are open and they're vulnerable right now, but they're together, away from everyone else. And that makes the healing process easier to endure.

The players react differently to the season's end. One or two are visibly relieved that it's all over but for the most part they feel the little death of dismissal very deeply.

Stephen Cunningham catches my eye and offers a little glance to the heavens. He sits in the corner with his head in his hands and promises himself this is the last time. There's bleak resignation all over his bruised features. As he takes in some fluids the stark reality hits home. This is full-time. In more ways than one. No more encores. He's spent the last 15 seasons devoting his every fibre to the cause and what's there to show for it? Just one lousy championship win.

One win in all that time. No more now. He's 33 and his back, hips and knees ache.

The dream? The dream is dead. Accept it, move on.

At least he can look himself in the mirror. And when he leaves the ground tonight and boards the team bus one last time he can walk away happy enough in his skin. He gave it all he could.

The same goes for the rest. They've been walking an uphill journey for a long time now but still they plough on. In fact, if anything, these guys are actually starting to create something of a legacy.

They're refusing to throw in the towel and slowly but surely they're breaking a vicious cycle. History has pigeon-holed Waterford football as a complete joke but in recent years this lot have rallied. They assembled a reasonable enough squad and probed hard for an escape route from the wastelands of Gaelic football. They came close to breaking out once or twice. In 2008, they were just about to flee Division 4 but tripped over at the final hurdle. In 2009, they raised the bar even higher, training 60 times from January to June to make their mark.

Respect however has been hard to come by. Recently they were described as a 'pub team' by one TV pundit and yet here they are sitting quietly, the real heroes of the GAA, playing for no reward or glamour. But keeping the show on the road all the same.

If 15 years of service for the likes of Cunningham only means that the team are no longer seen as village idiots, then so be it. It's something.

Tonight, though, you sense that one or two others are pondering their futures. It's taking so much to keep the thing going. You can't keep going back to the well time and again without some sweetener.

When you're down at this end of the scale nothing ever comes easy. Two days before the Meath game, John Kiely, Waterford's manager, noticed that the boots of a player were split and quizzed him about it. Months earlier the lad had been handed the boots courtesy of the county board but they'd disintegrated through wear and tear. He hadn't a job at the time and couldn't justify the luxury of splashing out on a new pair so he made do with what he had. It's laughable that this could happen to a senior intercounty GAA player in 2009 but he didn't moan. He got on with the job. Down here they always do. Kiely, the voice, if not the walking embodiment of Waterford football, took it upon himself to buy him a new pair.

Throughout the past five years Kiely has devoted his every waking hour to taking them from the cesspits, aided by a small band of loyalists who helped keep the flag flying. Sometimes, the commitment of his players left him speechless.

That's what this story is about.

Paul Ogle, one of Kiely's most trusted lieutenants, is hobbling around on crutches. Three years ago in 2006 he postponed surgery on a tumour so he could play a championship match against Kerry. Tonight, he missed the Meath game because of a torn cruciate ligament. It was his second ligament tear in just 15 months. Many others would have packed it in at word of the second prognosis. But Ogle's already plotting his return.

Then there's Ger Power sitting at the far side of the room packing his gearbag – not to be confused with the Waterford selector of the same name. Four hours after Waterford played Cork in the opening round of the Munster championship, he flew to Australia. Sadly, it wasn't for a holiday or a getaway, it was to help his girlfriend, Bríd, search for her missing brother in Sydney. That's what was on his mind on the opening Sunday of summer.

As Power finishes packing the O'Gorman brothers return from the showers. There are three of them on this squad, twins, Maurice and Thomas, and their younger brother, Michael. They lost their mother,

Kathleen, in July 2008 and their father, John, just eight months later. Somehow they have kept the show on the road, travelling to a league game in London just a week after John's passing. Fighters; an incredible family. In a time of adversity they remained the standard bearers of the team. In turn, playing for Waterford kept them going. No surrender.

As he heads for home you spot a wry smile appearing on Cunningham's face. Maybe it's a tinge of pride. Sometimes you take great solace from knowing that you kept the faith. That you finished the race. It is not a moral failing to be outplayed.

This is their story, the highs and lows they shared as the 2009 season unfolded. And there are plenty of both.

Remember, what you see on the pitch is only a fraction of what goes down.

Chapter 1
New Year, Same Goal

A New Year Begins
—•—

2 January, 2009, Kill, County Waterford

IT started like it always does, a frostbitten day that holds everyone prisoner indoors, picking at the leftovers of the Christmas just passed.

Around lunchtime, with his family settling down on the couch for the afternoon and a great fire blazing, Mick Ahearne cut his comforts and bade farewell. Carefully easing his car out of Kill and aiming it in the direction of Dungarvan, he began the first journey of a new season, the germination of another dream seeding in his mind.

After eight years trekking over and back to play football for Waterford, Ahearne could navigate this route in a blanket of darkness. Save for a blip in 2003, when frustration temporarily dampened his spirits, he's been the county's most consistent player this past decade. He's stood toe to toe with champion midfielders such as Darragh Ó Sé, Eamonn O'Hara and Nicholas Murphy, modern-day superstars of Gaelic football, and lived to tell the tale. His manager mostly refers to him as 'The Warrior' – which says it all.

Today, a new book opens and its pages are blank; he wants to put words on them himself. The first chapter unfolds at Fraher Field, where IT Tralee have arrived to play the first round of the McGrath Cup. It ain't Croke Park at the end of September and it never will be, but for Ahearne it's the birth of a new year. One more shot at the dream.

He fetches his gearbag from the car boot and feels a warm glow inside as he nears the dressing room. It will be nice to see them all again. The winter off-season has meant only sporadic bouts of training since last year, an odd spot of weight-pumping. But now he can hear the banter again – his second family.

Once inside, before making eye-contact with anyone, he runs a quick tally on the bodies, a reflex habit you pick up when you play a few years for Waterford. Not bad. There are 16 or so. 'Or so' means there might be 16 but there will probably be the bare 15. Finding a sub and getting him togged out on such Baltic days in January can demand extreme powers of persuasion. Some of the more stubborn guys keep their jeans on and their arms folded; the body language says 'Do not look in this direction'. The rest are either 'injured' or 'not quite fit enough yet'.

But Hurney is there and that's a good sign.

On his day, there's a touch of the Kieran Donaghys about Gary Hurney, the six-foot-four target-man who can catapult a team to greater heights from either full-forward or midfield. He's always in demand, always being dragged to and fro. This year again the county hurlers have sent him an SOS, but the footballers need him more. Much more. Waterford is that sort of county; apart from hurling loyalists Ballygunner, every club plays both codes. That suggests football receives healthy attention but Hurney's dilemma actually disproves that theory. In a place where the battle of the round ball meets with widespread apathy, the tug of war is heavily weighted toward one end. Always has been. This is a hurling county.

As Ahearne starts to tog out, team trainer Mick O'Loughlin summons the squad onto the field and coaxes them into the warm-up. The coach is all energy and enthusiasm, like a father introducing a young son to the joys of kicking a ball with the promise of great days ahead. Easing them through the pre-match drills, O'Loughlin makes the logical point that the sooner they get cracking, the sooner it will all be over. And so, with plenty of layers added for protection, it's out into the freezing cold as the first buds of the 2009 season push their way into the light.

Fraher Field is playable – just about. It's pockmarked with ragged holes and hollows, but it'll do. Today's game doubles as the official launch of the GAA's new experimental rules, which basically stipulate that if you look sideways at an opponent you're off. Yellow cards are expected to be passed around like cups of tea at a wake, and that explains the small army of sports photographers invading Dungarvan.

Still, the media frenzy has left the man and woman in the street conspicuously unmoved. Just 76 spectators, most of them parents of the visiting students, brave the elements. Faces ravaged with the cold, they dance furiously on the spot to get the blood circulating and exchange demented glances that speak louder than cries of anguish: 'What in the name of all that's holy are we doing here?'

Game on. The home side begin as if they have several points to prove this year. Sean Fleming, a diminutive corner-forward better known in these parts as 'Beag', bangs in two early goals and Hurney soon adds another to put his side eight points clear. Gradually, though, they run into oxygen debt, and by half-time, the younger, fitter college lads are back in contention: 3-7 plays 1-5. Waterford dig in and hang on, just about, to win by two points: 3-11 to 3-9. Notably, Tralee's brilliant full-forward David Culloty has posted 2-5. We'll definitely see him again.

Meanwhile, the college wing-back Joe Scully has seen yellow, thus becoming the first spring lamb in the country to be sacrificed on the altar of the new rules. And by the time Cillian O'Keeffe, one of the kids on the home team, follows him off, the photographers are long since packed up and on the road home. They have their shot. As for the final score? They couldn't give a hoot.

7

O'Keeffe's dismissal hands Sean Dempsey, the only sub on view, a run, but he looks less than eager. By now the cold has gathered an icy momentum and the chilled air is positively growling. You can't blame the lad for wanting to stay put.

Afterwards, in the relative comfort of the dressing room, Ahearne is grateful for a win they nearly let slip. 'We collapsed in the second half but we had absolutely nothing done and they were way fitter than us,' he says, nicely summarising the 60-odd minutes just gone.

From Fraher Field, team and management head to Lawlor's Hotel for a meal and a meeting to map out the year ahead. Down there, there are no grand boasts or targets set; they know better than that. No talk of reaching for the stars; sometimes they're wary of reaching for the ceiling for fear of deflation.

A modest chart of their 2009 campaign is handed out. For now, it's stamina work and coaching three nights a week – Mondays, Wednesdays and Fridays. There will be weight training with their specialist coach Mel Shanley on Thursdays and a match on weekends.

'Apart from getting an inkling of those plans there wasn't a whole lot more said,' Ahearne muses. 'The most important point was that fellas will be accounted for from now on. Sometimes, a lot of lads are missing and it ruins the whole thing. You'd be there bursting your arse but you'd leave demoralised because there were only 12 or 13 lads. It needs to be sorted.'

That's the only chunk of negativity you'll hear from him. He plays in a county where success is scarce but he doesn't need your pity. Nor do the others. They do this because they want to. Up to five years ago they were the laughing stock of Gaelic football, a circus act that trawled the by-waters of Ireland taking a pie-pounding from the locals of every town they visited, but they've stopped clowning about. Inch by inch, they've turned the guffaws into smiles of admiration and raised the bar a little higher every season. Bit by bit, they're getting to where they want to be. Division 3. That's the dream.

'We're no longer the clowns, that's for sure,' Ahearne says. 'We have players on the Munster team, we're improving every season, management are adding more and more to the set-up, but the most important thing is we have the same lads, more or less, that we've had for the past few seasons.

'Before, you could have an entirely different squad from year to year. No wonder we got nowhere. You'd train with a lad for 10 months and never see him again. John Kiely's first breakthrough as our manager was bringing in lads, his second was keeping them and his third achievement was getting some consistency.'

A glance around the room in Lawlor's shows how far they've come. Maurice O'Gorman and his twin, Thomas, won interprovincial medals with Munster last year; Ahearne, Liam Ó Líonáin and Hurney have reached that level in the past too. There are decent players to choose from.

That's down to Kiely, known here as 'Jackson' because of his admiration for the Confederate general of the same name from the American Civil War.

General Jackson was a tactical genius, and the Waterford manager has long since been a fan. He looks and acts a little like him too; a big, powerful man with a beard and a relaxed style of leadership who loved confusing opponents. Kiely ticks the same boxes.

In 2008, days before they played Carlow in the league, Kiely received a phone call from the former Dublin star Paul Bealin, a good friend who was managing Carlow at the time.

'Well, John, have ye much done?'

'Ah Jaysus, nothing, Bealo. We'd be doing well to get 11 or 12 lads out during the week. And yourselves?'

'Flying it. We have them in twice a week at 6 a.m. for training.'

'You're not serious!' Kiely responded, 'Jesus, some of our lads wouldn't turn up at 6 p.m.'

Bealin had his inside track.

'Ah grand, John. Sure I'll see you Sunday then.'

'No bother, Bealo.'

They 'communicated' again near the end of that league match. Waterford were eight points up with time running out. Jackson passed along the sideline near his opposite number and allowed himself a mischievious grin. 'Jaysus, Bealo,' he whispered, 'You'd want to leave those lads have a lie-in in the mornings. Dragging them out of the bed – 'tis doing them no good at all.'

All Bealin could manage was a rueful chuckle. He should have known better than to fall for the poor mouth.

In former times, Carlow would have wiped the floor with Waterford, but under Kiely things are seldom as expected. The truth is they're a safe distance from where he found them – marooned at a crossroads and en route to nowhere, lucky to win two games a season.

Rewind the clock to 2005, at his inaugural session in St Augustine's College, Dungarvan. Kiely could barely muster 12 players. They had five footballs, a small bit of interest and nothing else, no cones or equipment. The backroom team consisted of Paco Curran (coach), Ger Power (selector), Tom Condon (selector) and Mick O'Loughlin (trainer). There were no hangers-on or groupies. They were on their own.

At that time, intercounty football hardly registered. Fellas were too busy either hurling or playing club football, both of which offered considerably more potential than the Waterford football team.

Fast forward to 2009, though, and the new panel is already picked – and most of the faces from four years earlier are still in the mix. They have as many balls and cones as they want. The backroom team has expanded to also include Cian O'Connor as their physio, Johnny Grace as their masseur, Mel Shanley as the weights trainer and David Kenneally as the endurance trainer. Perhaps the biggest addition has been Paul McLoughlin, the ex-Kildare footballer recently drafted in as coach.

The manager has added an extra dimension to the camp with every passing campaign, but this time there's another challenge. For the past three years collective preparation started in the middle of November, providing them with a good base going into January. This year, though, with the winter training ban, they must hurriedly squeeze in as many sessions as they can.

'If every other county has adhered to the ban we should be okay, but I'm not sure they have,' Ahearne smiles knowingly. 'We'll find out soon enough. The main thing is that we're consistent this season and keep the likes of Gary Hurney. He wants to play both hurling and football but I'm not sure Davy Fitzgerald will see it like that. In fact, there's no chance he will. I can't even see Gary being with us for the league.'

Fitzgerald, the county's senior hurling manager, also has Hurney's two younger brothers, Patrick and John, on his books, not to mention Shane Walsh, another talented footballer who Kiely lost to hurling for the past four years. Without them, the consistency Ahearne craves will be hard to find.

'It might be, but hopefully we can build on last year when we won a string of matches,' he says. 'People might say that beating Clare in the Munster championship in 2006 was our highlight but while it was great, all I can remember is going out and getting a stuffing from Kerry the next day. No, the highlight of my time with Waterford was definitely the consistency of last year's league [2008]. We only missed promotion by a point and won five games in all. Only for Tipp catching us with two late goals in the last few minutes of our game we would have been promoted. That, by the way, was my lowlight.'

In any team it's hard to keep spirits constantly raised. Sometimes you feel like crawling back into the trenches and running up the white flag. Ahearne did just that back in 2003.

'I was sick of it,' he explains. 'Greg Fives, Denis Walsh, Billy Harty – they all came in as managers over a short space of time and gave it 100 per cent but we were going nowhere. The year out got me going again, and then Jackson came in with new players, most of whom have all stuck around. I mean, those O'Gormans are as good as you'd see anywhere and I'm glad the joke element has gone out of it now. We train seriously and work hard, and our league results over the past few years show that.

'Half our battle is getting lads to tog out – not many counties have that problem – and another big negative is that we have no one from the city on our squad. Out of 50,000 people there surely are a few footballers in there but we don't see them.

'So it's a small pool we have. There were times when we could have done with training under lights as well to improve our skills early in a season, but after the hurlers have finished dancing around and making shite of pitches in the county not many club officers want to let the footballers in too. Those are our challenges but we seem to get around them as much as we can.'

So far this year, Piltown, just outside Carrick-on-Suir, has been their home. The floodlights are good and not only can the players see each other, they can also manage some decent skills work.

Getting their hands on the ball is the most crucial aspect now. They are all relatively fit. Following the win over IT Tralee it's been decided to have three sessions the week after. By the time the next game arrives you can already see an improvement.

'Budgie' and the Limerick Students

11 January, Lemybrien, County Waterford

IT'S official: this is Ireland's coldest winter since 1991.
This time, Fraher Field is out of bounds, not because of the monsoon rains or the sheets of frost that have brought Ireland's roads and fields to a standstill, but because flocks of ravenous seagulls have destroyed the surface by relentlessly picking at it.

And so the magic of the McGrath Cup moves instead to Lemybrien, the home of Kiely's club, Kilrossanty, which has a field, floodlights and dressing rooms. It will do fine.

Limerick IT, better known for their hurling bloodline, are today's second-round opponents. They're young, fit and bulling for the road, but that's about it; no big names jump out from the LIT teamsheet (not that Kiely has too many at his disposal either).

All things considered, it should be an easy win for Waterford even in these brutal conditions.

Rain lashes down with a vengeance. Driven by a howling wind, it sweeps across the pitch. It's so cold the gate-checker doesn't even bother taking his hands out of his pockets to ask for a few shekels as you enter. The entrance fee is a princely €10 but with a measly 9 supporters coughing up, it's fair to assume the Munster Council are running this competition as a heavy lossmaker.

Michael Collins, who refereed the 2001 All-Ireland final between Galway and Meath, is down for this game. In the sanctuary of his dressing room he wraps himself up in 'under-armour gear' before taking a look outside and grimacing.

'It's bad but there's no danger of it being called off,' he says, much to the disgust of those present, not least his umpires, who face the likely prospect of being blown or even washed away by the storm.

You wonder how hard it is for Collins to motivate himself to handle non-events in such purgatorial conditions after experiencing the euphoric highs of running provincial and All-Ireland finals in front of 80,000 people.

'Look,' he says, 'the pace of the game is different from when the top counties play and obviously there's a dip in profile too, but if anything these games can be more demanding for refs. The weather is just brutal, it's always going to be hard to get any good football played and the tackling needs to be watched. Plus, we have the new rules, so there's more paperwork. But I spoke to both teams before the game and they know what to expect.'

In the end, only the midfielder Dermot Casey sees yellow in what proves to be the anticipated easy win. It finishes 1-14 to 0-5 and things are looking · up; the centre-forward Michael O'Gorman, a brother of those redoubtable twins, Maurice and Thomas, snaffles 1-5 in a man-of-the-match display and this time Kiely has the luxury of three subs to experiment with. We're into bonus territory here.

They could have done with a harder contest, mind. Before the game, Limerick IT had 'warmed up' for so long in the storm they could barely raise a gallop once the ball was thrown in. They never managed a score in the second half, though their midfielder Micheal Ó hAiliosa did put in a heroic afternoon's work.

Today, Kiely saw his left flank come alive through the industry of the wing-back Paul Ogle and wing-forward Stephen Cunningham, who took control of large swathes of the field, switching relentlessly between defence and attack when need dictated.

If you're looking for the living definition of 'stalwart' down here, Cunningham's your man. He spent time breaking bread with the county senior hurling panel under Gerald McCarthy in 1999 and 2000 but has been ever-present with the footballers since October 1995. Only Anthony Rainbow, Jason Sherlock, Paul McGrane, Darragh Ó Sé and Eamonn O'Hara are knocking around the intercounty scene longer. But all of them have experienced considerably more than one championship win in that time. Not Cunningham. Many others would have lost heart by now but he hasn't. At 33, he should be at full-forward directing the youngsters around him like a grizzled veteran but instead he skips up and down the field, revelling in the roving wing-forward role. Two years back, he was instructed, alongside Jason Ryan, to drift from attack to help form a blanket defence designed to limit damage on the scoreboard. Then Ryan left to take charge of Wexford and Cunningham has since been deployed as the lone extra defender. The brief is restrictive but doesn't prevent him poaching two points against the Limerick students.

14

They know him as 'Budgie' because of his slight frame and you could say he's their Brian Dooher, the kind of all-action guy that seems to have a twin brother on the pitch and can land a couple of points. More importantly, he's a leader; others look up to him.

'I'm fitter now that I ever was,' he says. 'I want to be on this team but to do the job I do, I have to be fitter than ever and I have to prove myself every year because Jackson has young lads coming in.

'I think we were robbed of promotion last year and it would be good to rectify that before I leave. It was just sickening not to get up to Division 3 and it took me a good while to come to terms with it, but I'm delighted to be back training and playing again even if I am on the home straight.

'These McGrath Cup games are fine, but it's the first round of the national league against Wicklow that we have to be right for,' he insists, looking down the road. 'That's a huge game. If we win we're capable of tacking on another three wins on the trot. That said, if we don't get a result I don't think there's a chance of us imploding either. Our league group will be so tight that any team could afford to lose two games and still get promoted. So for me, the McGrath Cup is all about building lads up so we can challenge Wicklow. We have University of Limerick next and while the games are great, I feel we need to play a county team soon. The colleges are fit but they're not physically strong enough to challenge you and their off-the-ball running isn't the same as what we'll face in February and March. The sooner we face intercounty sides the better.'

A management accountant, Cunningham got married last October, and will be busy this year combining football with a change of job and building a house. He's only recently recovered from a cartilage operation that ruled him out of last year's championship and has a lot to cram into the schedule.

'It's grand because things are looking up,' he says. 'The set-up is co-ordinated now and there are no dickheads or egos here. If there were, they wouldn't last too long.'

The Hurling Pull

—•—

18 January, Kill

ANOTHER brute of a day. The poor old gatekeeper has clearly been out in the weather too long; his face – like that of a coalminer or trawlerman – has physical hardship etched in every line.

Today, Lemybrien is unplayable, so the cabaret has moved to Kill. It's McGrath Cup semi-final time and UL, managed by up-and-coming trainer Cian O'Neill and coached by former Kerry goalkeeper and All-Ireland medal winner Declan O'Keeffe, are blocking Waterford's path to the final.

The teams gather in the small village about 13 miles outside Waterford city and tog out in the community centre before jogging across the road to the pitch and warming up. There are a few cars on each side of the road and this time a whopping total of 107 fans have turned up, although it's hard to figure out who they're supporting because there's not a handclap to be heard as the game progresses.

The squad, or at least those who turned up, have trained hard, shimmying between the physical stuff and ball work three nights a week. Half the panel have been putting in weights sessions with Shanley. Their legs are weary but another match will do them no harm at all and a final place against Cork, their championship opponents later this season, beckons. Finals don't grow on trees down here; they'd take it.

David Moran, the promising Kerry star and son of the legendary Ogie, is picked to play at full-forward but Kiely reckons he has that threat already nullified. The plan is fiendishly cunning. Sort of.

'I'll be putting one of the O'Gormans on him to man-mark him,' he states, as he studies the match programme. 'I just haven't decided which one to put on him yet.'

It seems that for every mini-crisis in Kiely's managerial career 'putting one of the O'Gormans on him' is the solution.

In the end, though, Moran doesn't play and so the sticky services of the brothers are deployed elsewhere, sparing Kiely the toil of a tactical duel with O'Keeffe.

The manager has already scouted UL and saw them play the McGrath Cup quarter-final against WIT. He knows they play a two-man full-forward line and depend on short kick-outs to get them going.

It turns out his pre-match report was spot-on but unfortunately his players didn't pay enough heed. Near the end, they trail by seven points and frustrations are boiling over. Paul Ogle has defended tirelessly throughout the match and has been engaged in a running battle with the UL midfielder Fiachra Lynch. After a few minor fouls he gets a yellow card from referee Brian Tyrell and is ordered off.

Having put so much into the game he's absolutely disgusted at getting his marching orders.

'Jesus, that's bullshit!' he roars as he reaches the dug-out. 'He's a diver. Bullshit!'

Minutes later, centre-back Eddie Rockett experiences the same sinking feeling when he also gets the line as tensions almost boil over again. Before being sent off, Rockett had been involved in one of the game's lighter moments. He sprinted forward from the half-back line and after an electric four-man move took the ball on an overlap. Darting past the 45-metre line he glanced up and directed a missile toward the top left-hand corner of the net. For the only time that day the crowd gasped in unison as the ball prepared to take the net with it. Then, at the last moment, it took a vicious left turn and walloped off the post.

Cue hoops and howls of demented laughter from the Waterford subs, who sprang from the bench and doubled up with delight as the unlucky Rockett set about the lonely odyssey home to centre-back. They celebrated as if they were bullfighters chosen from thousands to run in Pamplona.

'We'd never have heard the end of it,' one explains, as the excitement dies down.

Meanwhile, Kiely scratches his head, perplexed at the miss. 'Mother-a-Jaysus, how in the name of God did that stay out?' he asks no one in particular.

Inspired by Rockett's near-heroics, the team rally and pull a couple of scores back before submitting by 5 points, 0-13 to 0-8, in the end. Quite simply, they had no answer for UL's go-to guy, Enda Varley, a rare specimen in that he's from Mayo and holds an All-Ireland medal from the 2006 U-21 final. Today, the left-footed assassin shoots 0-7 in an exhibition.

It was a fair result. Waterford's goalkeeper Tom Wall had to brilliantly save a penalty from Lynch, but at the other end Kiely's men hit the post twice. For most of the second half, though, they were clueless in attack and for some strange reason kept bouncing the ball on a surface that had as much resistance as the marshes of Sliabh Luachra.

It didn't help that Maurice O'Gorman spent the half-time break vomiting and had to be switched to the forwards in the second half because there simply wasn't enough cover on the bench to replace him. There they had only three subs togged, young lads who would have been blown away by either the opposition or the elements.

To compound their misery Hurney has indicated he's sticking with the hurlers for 2009. Shane Walsh is staying with them too. Both were expected to make today's football game but it didn't happen. Davy Fitzgerald has told Hurney he has big plans for him; the football selectors remain unconvinced but they're powerless to do much about it. If they were in Hurney's shoes they would probably choose the same path.

'Ah there's only so much chasing you can do,' Kiely sighs as his players warm down under the watchful eye of Paul McLoughlin. 'Those lads would be great additions but we were short another six or seven apart from them today. We'll just have to get on with it. And I'll tell you, we have some amount of work to do. We worked them hard in training last week but they'll have to go harder now.

'Still and all I'm happy. There were years we would go an entire season without winning a game and now we've won two before the end of January. Two or three lads are playing great stuff and we'll have a challenge against

Waterford IT and Dromcollogher-Broadford before we look at Wicklow. 'Twould have been nice to have reached a final but we didn't do too bad with what we have.'

Right now he's short the services of last year's entire full-back line and another six or seven are recovering from injury.

'But sure that's the challenge and I love it,' he shrugs. 'I don't get anything out of this only personal satisfaction. There's no money – I wouldn't take a bob. We were playing a match last year and the opposing manager was joking about how he had nice electronic gates fitted at home with the few bob he was getting from training the team. He asked me what I got. I told him I'd got a mobile home. I think he believed me.'

Right now, though, Kiely's biggest problem isn't fretting over a few quid, it's getting the players out training.

Mel the Motivator

Mel Shanley, a former prop and All-Ireland winner with Clonakilty Rugby Club, knows at first hand the problems that exist in that regard. Each Thursday the sturdy Dungarvan native opens the doors of his Nip and Tuck studio to Kiely's team. Well, to some of them anyway.

Last year, he had a core bunch of around 6 or 7 sticking to his programme; this year the average has been 12 or 13. In any other county, weight training would be mandatory but in Waterford the management know that if they push too hard they won't see some lads again and won't have a squad to pick from.

Hence, while the team is encouraged to seek out Shanley there is no direct order.

'I would say some players would rather do their own programme, others feel my way is not as good as theirs and there would be one or two who would probably say, "What would that fat hoor know about it – look at the size of him?"' he quips light-heartedly.

A weightlifting expert, Shanley is currently taking the strength and conditioning course run by Dr Liam Hennessy and Jim Kilty, the internationally renowned athletics coach. In his studio there are no machines, only free weights. The team do squats, dead lifts, snatches and Olympic weightlifting to get the whole body working. His sessions last no longer than 45 minutes; any more than that, he reckons, is a waste of time.

'I would love to see the whole panel row in with me but on the field you can really tell the guys who are putting in the strength work,' he says. 'They are the guys who can keep going for 70 minutes – Mick Ahearne, Paul Ogle, Stephen Cunningham, John Hayden, Liam Ó Líonáin, people like that.

'The O'Gormans were in once or twice but they are exceptional characters and I have to ask myself is there really anything I could do with them to improve them. Sometimes there's a lot to be said for the saying, "If it ain't broken, don't fix it".

'Other lads come in, see how to do things and head off to do it on their own because they live 30 miles away from the studio in Dungarvan. It suits them better, which is fair enough too.'

Gradually, Shanley has become fascinated with the whole set-up. Although introduced solely to help the squad with weights, he now finds himself attending most of their matches and some of their physical training sessions. He offers advice on hydration and nutrition and throughout the McGrath Cup campaign he uncovered some interesting snippets which he relayed to the manager.

'I weigh the players before and after every game or training session and I monitor the results,' he says. 'One lad lost four kilos against IT Tralee and that's worrying. It means he lost 9 or 10 pounds of fluids, which means he wasn't fully hydrated. The average player on the team is losing at least one kilo at the moment and that's not good enough because in my book they're supposed to put weight on during games, not lose it.

'I think that 48 hours before a game they need to be tucking into their pasta with white mushroom sauce and chicken breasts to load up on carbohydrates and they need to sip on three litres of water a day but many of them are leaving it until the day of a match to do all this and it's way too late.

'I need to speak to them on the nutrition side of things again and I've told Jackson that. If I'm being honest, it's 20 per cent of the lads who are doing 80 per cent of the work and in a squad environment that's not good enough.

'But it's not for me to be crowing on about it. In other counties, players will find it's compulsory to do this type of training but here you have to tread carefully to keep the players.'

Shanley reckons a ton of work needs to be done in the coming weeks and he's not the only one. Kiely is busy arranging challenge matches. McLoughlin is finalising a defence-orientated system, bearing in mind the missing bodies in attack.

But most of all they need settled numbers and decent turnouts at training.

'Accountability is what we need now,' Ahearne agrees. 'It's no good a lad not coming training and turning up for matches; I'd rather it was the other way around. We need to know where lads are if they are not training. Obviously, with players like Liam Lawlor, who's in college in Edinburgh, we know and understand his story, but we need everyone kicking in.'

'A rising tide lifts all boats,' Shanley adds. 'Get the players who want to play – and I still reckon there are a few more out there who have not been discovered – do the work and it will all come together.'

As for Kiely, he's seen it all before and refuses to panic. After a lifetime spent trying to lift the lethargy that clouds Waterford football, he knows bad habits are like a comfortable bed – easy to get into but hard to get out of.

Time to get back on the phones and lift morale, time to cajole lads back into the spirit of the thing.

It's what he does best.

Chapter 2
Jackson

A General's Sense of History

AN icy winter's evening in Dungarvan. Jackson sucks the life from another cigarette and clouds the air with a heavy sigh. Rubbing his hands to spark up some heat he bounds through the entrance of Lawlor's Hotel, throws off his jacket and begins processing a myriad of thoughts.

The hotel is sleepy but it seems to come to life when he passes through the soft lamplight of the lounge. Within seconds he's spinning the yarns, pausing only to wheeze a hearty laugh before dishing out the next anecdote. There's a fair depth to that cackle – 20 Major a day will do that to you.

The cold has reddened his cheeks and having spent hours scouring the county, chasing farmers for outstanding cheques, this builder is glad to take refuge. Tracking money in these dark times of recession is about as satisfying as seeing your mortgage repayments fall only for tax rates to rise. Still, judging by the look on his face, it's been a good day's work. Someone, somewhere must have coughed up.

He runs over the history of Waterford football and though there's not much to brag about, dates and results stream out of his mouth like tributaries flow into the Colligan. When it comes to anything to do with Gaelic football, he just can't help himself.

Nobody has a bad word to say about the guy. He kills cynicism. Whether talking to a binman or a neuro-surgeon, Kiely would hold his own. It may not mean much to the outside world but down here he's the most successful figure in the history of Waterford football, a beacon to guide others from the shadows.

In a county where national titles are equally scarce in both hurling and football, he has delivered two All-Ireland junior championships as manager and ended a 19-year famine without a win in the Munster senior championship. You get the picture!

People find it hard to say 'no' to him which is never a bad card to have in your repertoire. In terms of business he's self-made, having carved out a niche in the farm-building sector. Away from that, he likes the horses. And the quizzes. Over the years he's taken on all the top TV shows, won a few bob and the odd holiday from each of them – *Murphy's Micro Quiz-M, Top Score, Where in the World.* The lot.

As he settles down to recount the pretty awful record of football in these parts, he openly admits there's little to get revved up about. Yet he has plenty of stories to recount. About anything and everything. It's best just to let him at it.

'You'd run over our past very quickly,' he says. 'The one thing I will say is that while we in Waterford football might be regarded as also-rans we have a serious history. When the seven men founded the GAA in Thurles, Waterford were the first county in Ireland to have a proper championship. That was in 1885; you won't find that in any other county. Ballysaggart won the final that year and my own club Kilrossanty took part in it.

'Back then we were big hitters,' he reflects. 'In 1886 and 1887 we were doing well in Munster, reaching finals, but we reached the All-Ireland final in 1898, losing to Dublin. Gaelic football was played on a regular basis all through the 1890s, right up to the First World War. Hurling only took off in the early 1920s when Erins Own emerged with a super team with Mount Sion after them. There's a lot of shite talked about the status of football in this county but there was no hurling final played in Waterford until 1897, 12 years after the first football final.'

In the 1950s there was reasonable progress. Kerry only beat them by three points in Munster and the minnows actually whipped the Kingdom in 1957 with eight Kilrossanty players on board. They mustered a team, got their boots on and went out and beat a county chasing its nineteenth All-Ireland title. It's still considered the greatest day in Waterford football history. Three years later they beat Cork in the 1960 Munster final and managed to gain Division 2 status. Glory days.

But like a Bank of Ireland share, their stock peaked and then nose-dived. They've been freefalling since.

The 1980s were average and the 1990s septic. By the time the new millennium rolled into town Waterford football was irrelevant. Save for two unexpected wins against Kerry in the Munster U21 championship, one in 2000 and another which delivered a provincial title in 2003, a county with proud footballing origins had fallen off the radar.

There were those who tried to navigate them back to dry land. Greg Fives, Kiely's best friend who passed away in October 2008, did all he could to keep the flame burning but it was like negotiating a winding hill only to find a mountain ahead. Upon taking the reins of the senior team Fives decided to seek counsel. He rang Dublin legend Kevin Heffernan for advice.

Not readily associated with gestures of affection, there was no mistaking the disdain in Heffernan's voice when he lifted the phone at the other end.

'Who the bleedin jaysus is this?' he growled.

'Greg Fives,' came the reply, 'I'm just after taking over the Waterford football team. Have you any advice for me?'

'I have,' Heffo barked. 'Resign.'

Boosted by that shot in the arm from one of the game's greatest managers, Fives thought long and hard about seeking nuggets from anyone else. But he kept going.

One day he asked Kiely to help prepare the team for a league match away to Sligo. Now, you could dickie it up as a manager spreading his wings and seeking technical advice from a wily observer – or you could explain that the rest of Fives' selectors had decided Sligo was way too far to travel for a match and so it was left to Jackson to oblige. Either way, there's a nice yarn to tell.

'We were in the dressing room up there and Greg had a terrible short fuse,' Kiely recollects. 'He was screaming and shouting, telling lads what we needed was men with *liathróidís*. He was thumping the walls and wasn't there a nail sticking out of the wall and next thing his hand stuck to it. Jesus, the laughing we did.

'Another day we took the team on a 1982 bus to Derry for a league game but sure the bus couldn't even get up the hill in Dungarvan town. It cranked out before we reached the top of the road. Everyone ended up driving. The county board put the boys up in a hotel in Donegal because it was cheaper. They had to drive to Derry the next morning. It would have been quicker to walk from Dungarvan the day before. I think Derry scored 5-32 that afternoon.'

But through it all their spirit remained intact. In 2004, they enjoyed perhaps the biggest hoot of them all.

Kiely was preparing the county for a junior All-Ireland semi-final against Lancashire. They'd beaten Cork in the Munster final but as much as they enjoyed that result, the idea of heading over to Manchester, reaching an All-Ireland final and hitting the town for the night was way more enticing.

'Cork were sick as parrots, they had the weekend in Manchester booked before they even played us – they were so sure of beating us,' he remembers. 'That trip was all about Paddy O'Grady from The Nire. He was buried about a month after Greg. What a great man! Anyway, Michael Burns, our corner-back, decided to fly over to the UK from Cork, while the rest of us flew from Dublin. Paddy had been involved in football all his life and asked to take Michael's place on the flight from Dublin. We had no problem with that and so Paddy took Michael's seat and off we went, arriving and then checking into Jury's Hotel, Manchester.

'Of course the real Michael turned up later and needed his sleep for the match, so when Paddy turned in around 4 a.m. he had to sleep on a chair in Michael's room. We went out, won the match well and had a mighty night together but before we knew it, 'twas time to come home. For pure devilment, David Ryan, the other corner-back, put a big carving knife in Paddy's hand luggage as we left the hotel.

'Paddy went through the metal detection place and every light in the airport went off. All hell broke loose. Bin Laden wouldn't have got a reception like it. He was stopped by police and in a panic he told them his name was Michael Burns. But sure then all the boys on the team started shouting "Paddy this and Paddy that" at him. He couldn't even look at them for fear of breaking down laughing. Michael had already gone through security and yet all over the world I'd say every sort of a check was being run on him. They thought they had some sort of terrorist. Then Paddy told them his real name and the police were really stumped. We told them he suffered from dual personality and sure they wouldn't let any of us on the flight then. We had to get out home on the next one.'

Jackson and the Junior Job

Eventually it was Jackson's turn to up the ante and take the job, but even in a county where football was the punchline in every wag's joke he was forced to serve the most humble of apprenticeships. He helped as a junior selector in 1998 to Tom Cunningham, Stephen's father, and got a taste for it.

'At the end of '98, we had little to show for our troubles and I went to the county board chairman, Paddy Joe Ryan, and asked him for the junior job. I told him straight out that we'd win an All-Ireland the following year.'

Ryan thought Kiely was after a feed of magic mushrooms but all the same he knew the boundless energy which this man flaunts would have terrible repercussions for slackers all over the county. Kiely got the gig.

The fact that there weren't too many standing in his way is lost on him. As far as he was concerned he had the job of his dreams. It proved to be a fine move for Waterford; they'd won two All-Ireland senior football titles in a different lifetime but zilch in the 100 years since. By the time Jackson moved on to the senior team he had delivered two All-Ireland junior crowns for the county.

He remembers every leg of the '99 journey. Two weeks before they were due to play Cork he called a training session but no one turned up. Growing anxious, he contacted a friend of his in Cork, Mickey Walsh, to arrange a challenge against Imokilly a week later. Trying to get any sort of a decent player was a nightmare and they got duly slaughtered. That evening, Kiely openly questioned his sanity in taking the job. But he didn't despair.

Purely out of friendship, a few players helped out and came on board. Peter Queally finished hurling for the season and joined up too.

'Mickey offered up prayers for me because he feared for us against Cork,' Kiely smiles. 'And maybe he was right. But within a few days of that match we had a few more warriors on board and I felt differently about things. There was no proper effort being put in at senior level and some guys saw that and joined us. Others were overlooked and had a point to prove. Me? I just wanted warriors and in Queally, Shane Bergin and a few more I got them. Johnny Cummins from Tipperary, Brendan's father, was training the seniors and Cork beat them by 30 points in the Munster championship. He was devastated, but I brought him in with the juniors and it helped soften the blow for him.'

Somehow they beat Cork, who, like in every grade, boasted decent players such as the established Fachtna Collins who had played for years with the seniors. At the end of play, the scoreboard read 2-8 to 0-12. Mickey Walsh is still trying to figure out what happened in Fraher Field that evening.

Next up were Limerick. By now Waterford had added another talent in Niall Geary and whipped their opponents easily enough to reach the

Munster final against Clare. Trailing at half-time in that one, Kiely finally had an excuse to bring Queally onto the field.

'We'd a good spirit built up and Peter was only back from the hurling so I was careful not to start him in case it disrupted the team,' he explains. 'But we were down a few points and Colm Clancy was cleaning up for Clare. We needed him.

'I said: "Queally, the first thing you do when the ref throws in the ball is plant Clancy one and start a row." The year before, all hell had broken loose between Waterford and Clare in the Munster hurling final and I knew we could agitate Clare. Queally planted him one alright and somehow Clancy got booked. After that we had them rattled.'

They won again that day and in the All-Ireland semi-final put up a pretty fine display against Roscommon to win by six points. They brought 5,000 supporters with them to the final against Meath and within 10 seconds of the throw-in those die-hards were celebrating a goal. Early signs were good. Connie Power was on frees and slotted them over from all angles. At the end, with time just up, the scores were level when the Meath goalkeeper, still not believing that they hadn't Waterford put to the sword, tried a quick kick-out only to find his wing-back wasn't on the same wavelength. It trailed harmlessly over the line.

'My nephew, Jacko Kiely, was one of the heroes of that team,' the manager recalls. 'And out he waddled to take the line-ball. I said to kick it hard and wide, that we'd beat the shit out of them in the replay, but he replied: "No, look at David Ryan."'

Kiely looked 40 yards across field and sure enough there was Ryan, in a safe quarter behind enemy lines, spluttering out the last litre of dirty petrol on a rare voyage of discovery from corner-back into nosebleed territory. He fetched the ball into his hands, mustered just enough strength to send it over the bar and duly wrote himself into the history books with a majestic point.

The place exploded like a river bursting its banks. O'Moore Park was flooded in a swathe of white and blue. One neighbour of Kiely's got so excited that he became entangled in the wire in front of the stand. He was old and keyed up and they had to get a ladder to bring him down. Most of the team didn't make it home that night and instead there was a big reception the following evening on an open-top bus. The big time.

'We had mighty fun altogether,' Jackson recalls, 'but I didn't enjoy the celebratory ride from Abbeyside to Dungarvan at all because we had a character on the team who was langered and I was holding on to him because he wanted to jump off the bus.'

Eventually, Kiely talked the player down and persuaded him that it was better to keep kicking football than endure a year with his bones in a cast. As if seeing a sudden apparition in front of him, the player saw some logic in that and was still playing for Kiely in 2004 when they did the trick all over again, winning their second All-Ireland title.

'We had a slightly longer preparation for that one,' Jackson, now boasting a Mourhino-like strut, recollects.

'We beat Limerick in the Munster final and I had a strong team. Big Roger Power was still there, Michael Burns was captain; my full-back and goalkeeper were still there, David Ryan, Jacko, Eamon Doherty and Sean Dempsey too. I went for as many lads over six foot as possible; height and strength are a big advantage at junior level, you see. Mattie Kiely, one of the best Waterford footballers over the past 15 years, was eligible too because he hadn't played senior in 2003.'

Along the way, they beat another tasty-looking Cork team with future stars in tow like Alan Quirke, Alan O'Connor, John Hayes and Ger Spillane. On the day of the match, Kiely stopped in Middleton for a cup of tea and picked up the *Evening Echo* and read where all and sundry were predicting by how much Cork would hammer Waterford. Cashman bookmakers had Kiely's men at 13/2 to win and Cork at 1/10 so Jackson paid them a visit on the way home.

That night his team carved out another good win. And he collected one great bet.

By the end of the Munster campaign he had the luxury of giving every one of his 24-man squad a run-out. It's usually for different reasons that so many Waterford footballers get a chance in a campaign – because everyone else has walked away. Not this lot; they hammered Lancashire and played the All-Ireland final against Leitrim as a curtain-raiser to the Clare/Kilkenny All-Ireland hurling quarter-final, where the Henry Sheflin/Gerry Quinn affair stole all the headlines.

In the shadow of the media frenzy that centred on hurling's biggest name controversially picking up an eye injury, it was hardly noticed that the junior football final ended in a draw with the replay down for Birr the following week. But Kiely and Waterford didn't give one hoot about the hurling match; they had their own cry for justice to be heard. In the drawn game Jackson was convinced Leitrim fielded three ineligible players who had lined out for the county's senior team against New York but he decided to keep stum. The trio in question all played again in Birr which made the subsequent win all the sweeter.

Somewhere in the middle of another closely-fought rematch he lost his keeper, Anthony Kirwan, and as he didn't believe in carrying a sub goalie at junior level he threw Anthony Power into the breach. The reasoning? As good as any. Power had previously played in goal for a local soccer team.

But the deputy net-minder was as nervous as Willie O'Dea at a Dell Reunion Party and within a few moments he'd dropped two balls. Even at junior level you'll be punished for that.

Bang, bang. Two goals.

Kiely quickly made towards his stand-in goalkeeper, keen to deliver some well-intentioned gems of wisdom and support.

'I went in to him and said: "If you drop another one I'll fucking kill ya, I'll actually go in and beat the fuckin' head off ya myself."'

That delicious slice of man-management worked. Power openly admitted to his teamates afterwards that Kiely had 'frightened the shit out of him'.

Eventually, he was stabilised between the posts and Waterford surged ahead, kicking some massive points to win 2-12 to 2-9, coincidentally the same tally they'd reached in the 1999 final. Champions again. This time even hoary old cynics grew a wee bit misty-eyed at his achievements.

Raising the Bar

Inevitably, he came under huge pressure to take the senior job but was too heavily involved at club level and so he deferred the job until 2006. 'I thought long and hard about it even then,' he maintains. 'I needed a loyal backroom first of all. I put that in place and along the way I've made one or two changes.'

He walked into a camp full of club cliques and discord. But you don't so much talk to Kiely as enlist in his cause. It wasn't long before he created harmony.

All the usual problems that incorporate life in the wastelands affected them. In the early days tactical naivety cost the team valuable league points. There was the time they failed to man-mark Tipp genius Declan Browne in a league game and the Moyle Rovers man destroyed them by creating two goals while they stood back and admired him. But they learned. Now when they play, they crowd their defence, blunt the opposition's star man and attack en masse.

Some of their best players will always be committed to the hurlers and then there are the usual domestic complexities. Stradbally and The Nire have dominated the county championships, but their men – and the rest – haven't always linked up well with the county team, as defender Paul Ogle testifies.

'You'd come in sometimes, you'd train with a lad for five months and never see him again,' he says, recalling times passed. 'He could be with a junior club and that might be the last you'd see of each other. Some guys are primarily hurlers and others would have pucked the faces off each other in club games and held grudges. Jackson came in and made fellows from different clubs share rooms together and kept the same core of lads together. It's much better now, you can make progress.'

This year, there are six players from The Nire and two from Stradbally, but before Kiely took over players came and went like councillors in local elections. They grew disillusioned with hammering after hammering.

Such traffic in and out of the dressing room made it impossible to field a competitive team. For instance, of the U-21 team that unexpectedly won the 2003 Munster football final, only two are current seniors. But under Kiely, decent hurlers like Eddie Rockett and Liam Lawlor all returned to the fold. Along with Mick Ahearne, Brian Wall, Wayne Hennessy and Ger Power they now form the backbone of the team.

During Kiely's tenure, the seniors' main achievement has been ending a famine that spanned almost two decades without a championship win. In 2007, they finally rectified that damning statistic by beating Clare, who were in serious development mode at the time. Two seasons earlier they had spent €40,000 training in the Catskills Mountains in New York preparing for the start of that championship. Waterford scarcely spent that much all year. Their defeat of Páidí Ó Sé's side ultimately ended the Kerry hero's reign in the Banner. The media latched on to that win in a big way and for a while Waterford were Accrington Stanley or Kidderminister, lowlights who had put one over Manchester United. For a day or two, they were splashed all over the papers. That may have had something to do with the fact that Jackson wore a Glasgow Rangers FC jersey to a post-match media briefing. Anything for devilment.

But looking back, it was only a quick fix. It was a brutal game where both teams played rubbish and Waterford were destroyed by Kerry in front of the TV cameras weeks later. It took from the sweetness of a rare win from their mouths and instead left a sour tang.

The bar's raised a lot higher these days.

*   *   *

Under Kiely's guidance, opposing teams have to sweat hard to take anything off them. In the past two seasons they've beaten Cavan, Sligo, Antrim and Wexford in the league. They don't fight with each other anymore and they're competitive. Last year was their closest call, they missed out on promotion by a point but four of their players subsequently made the interprovincial squad, for which Kiely was a selector.

Making a Munster team is a big deal in these parts but there was still room for a bit of craic.

Maurice O'Gorman, an unknown quantity to the outside world, but one of the best man-markers on home soil, was one of those called up by Munster boss Ger O'Sullivan for provincial duty. But he was working in Wales and couldn't make it over and back for training. Not wanting to jeopardise his chances of making the team, Kiely sent his identical twin Thomas to training instead.

In Thomas went and cleaned up in the trials. In the end, both twins made the squad and had quite an impact. Where else would you get it?

Everyone has a story about the manager. In 2006 he arrived at Fraher Field for a league game with Carlow. Mick O'Loughlin takes up the tale.

'Liam Hayes was Carlow manager and turned up in a spanking BMW with a driver and gracefully walked by us with a clipboard in his hand, saluting us very politely. Next thing our man tears into the ground in an oul tow truck, abandons it, throws a fag out of his gob, strides over and let's a big "How'rye lads" before opening another box of Major on which he had the team picked and written. Some contrast.'

That same season in 2006 Kiely summoned The Yank into action.

Kevin Power came from San Francisco but upon retracing his roots, visited Ireland and joined Rathcormack GAA club. He settled in quickly, made the club juniors and then the seniors. He was athletic and not half bad with ball in hand. It didn't matter that he grew up in a different country; Kiely quickly deemed him good enough for the team. He started against Kerry in the 2006 championship.

But it's not a one-man show – far from it. The backroom team is now bursting at the seams. Making Division 3 is the common aim. As a group under Kiely's tenure, this might be the last chance they'll get to make that leap.

'It's our number one target; we should be in Division 3 already,' the boss reckons.

'We won five games last year, lost to Tipp in the last minute and effectively handed them the game. We played Offaly who had a huge scoring rate and they beat us by two points. But we had 13 wides. Same against Wicklow, where we hit four balls off the upright. Those games cost us. Then we go up and beat Antrim away from home. Jesus. We have the potential but I badly want to get out of where we are.'

Kiely's done a lot, but he's supping in the last-chance saloon. At the end of 2009, bar he delivers promotion, his love affair with the team might be culled. He's been five years in the job but the powers that be are becoming more demanding.

Late in 2008, there was talk of Cork U-21 winning coach Tony Leahy and former Tipp manager Johnny Owens being approached to play a part but the word is that when Kiely was informed that other names were in the mix, his reply was simple.

'Ah no, I'll be looking after things this year.'

End of discussion.

It's ironic; in raising the bar Kiely has set new standards for Waterford football.

By which he will now be judged.

Chapter 3
The Road to Deliverance

The Walking Wounded
—•—

11 a.m., 24 January, Dungarvan, County Waterford

St Augustine's College on the hub of Dungarvan. A Saturday morning with frost on the ground and football in the air. It's bitter and biting cold but there are 20 Waterford footballers running around, happy as ewes in spring, speeding through a seamless motion of drills and exercises.

Today is all about honesty. There's a general acknowledgement that things need to pick up quickly. The coaches are starting to bark and the players are bitching at each other, becoming more vocal as the morning progresses. It's all good; this is a sign of focus. They are beginning to work together with a common vision.

But there are one or two hitches.

Training is scheduled for 11 a.m. but it's at least 15 minutes past before all players are accounted for. After twiddling his thumbs waiting on the paddock, Paul McLoughlin eventually loses patience and decides enough is enough. He strides into the dressing room and berates the slackers for their poor timekeeping. They're taken aback; this is the first time they've seen their new coach lose it. Secretly though, the senior guys are delighted. The hairdryer treatment is exactly what's needed. Today, they reckon,

35

McLoughlin has shown who is in charge.

When they eventually kick off, the tempo is high and all cogs of the engine switch into operation mode. In the fog, Tom Condon, their long-serving selector, sets off on a long run, pounding the hardened ground while the team are put through their paces. One hour and exactly seven miles later, he returns to the dressing room, where those injured and unable to train are receiving physio. Condon had better stay fit; with so many walking wounded around, he could yet be needed for active service.

Players trickle in and out of the dressing room as the session unfolds. There's a pretty drastic injury crisis already and the selectors don't want to add to it by pushing the remaining crew too hard so they're careful not to flog anyone who is struggling.

For the great survivors who take part in The Full Monty, however, it's a demanding session, based mostly on stamina, speed and ball work. You can tell a mile off that Stephen Cunningham, even nearing his mid-30s, is fitter than most of his colleagues. This guy shows remarkable stomach for wading through the cesspit year after year.

Before each drill, Mick O'Loughlin dots the pitch with cones and bollards. He's combining very well with Paul McLoughlin and the players have picked up on that rapport. O'Loughlin, Deputy Principal at Presentation Secondary School Clonmel, hails from Tipperary but for the past four years he's devoted his heart and soul to Waterford football. In many ways he's the man who makes them tick, a logistics officer as well as a physical trainer.

Breaking away from the group for a few moments he offers his tuppence worth. It's good and bad; he's happy enough with the way things have gone so far but is equally concerned at the amount of work still to be done before the Wicklow game.

Being involved with a team like this can seem a thankless task but O'Loughlin is a realist and plays the hand he's dealt. Although there are 20 players at training, he knows most of their top men are elsewhere. But he prefers to focus on those who are making the effort.

'I'm happy with the fact that we won two matches in the McGrath Cup, considering we hadn't won a game in that competition for the last four years,' he explains. 'Then there was the opportunity to blood new players like Conor McGrath, Michael O'Gorman and John Hayden, which was beneficial.

'But we have a small panel and the injuries are killing us,' he adds. 'It's easy to identify our problems. No county can afford to lose the number of footballers we've waved goodbye to. It's a killer, but we have to get on with it and our main focus now is Wicklow.

'From here on we get game-specific. We have to increase our fitness levels, return to our system that gets 12 men behind the ball, try and sort a team and game-plan for that match. And hopefully, we'll get some challenge matches and settle on a team.'

With that he dashes away to help Paul McLoughlin take the team through the next segment of drills. Throughout, Jackson maintains a watching brief, calmly ambling the perimeter of the field, encouraging, scribbling notes, calling players out for a word here and there.

Power's Struggle

One of the injured, Ger Power, strolls out to take a look at proceedings before heading back to the dressing room for more physio with Cian O'Connor, their sports-injury specialist. A dual player, Power spent two seasons with the hurlers before reverting to Jackson's regime.

Nine years ago the Stradbally man scored the winning goal against Kerry in the Munster U-21 semi-final and he's also enjoyed a huge return with his club in recent years. Numbers may be down in training but his comeback is a massive boost. He is now 29, and his early comeback from a cruciate injury has been impressive.

He's fed up talking about it, but politely tells the tale one more time. They were playing Carlow in 2008's league when his leg stuck in a divot and gave way. He knew he was in trouble but played on because the knee didn't blow up. Medial ligament, he reckoned.

After visiting the surgeon Tadhg O'Sullivan, he discovered it was more serious than that. The knee hadn't blown up. It had blown out. Goodbye for 12 months.

'I had myself convinced that it wasn't the cruciate,' he smiles ruefully as he rewinds the memory slowly and deliberately.

'I had knee problems when I was 19 and knew a few things about them but I certainly didn't feel like I had done the cruciate. Jackson got me into Tadhg, who is the best in the business, and he said the knee was in a right state. I was down in the dumps but immediately after the operation I turned positive again – it was sink or swim. I knew I would come back strong and just decided to put the hard work in. Six weeks after the injury I was back running. My legs are strong from farming anyway and I was able to run and squat.'

He went under the knife on 22 May and rebuilt the strength in the knee up to Christmas. The dark winter nights of October and November should have seen him resting in front of the TV but instead he was back training with the club and taking it bit by bit, knowing that one sharp turn and the knee would implode again.

He ploughed a lone furrow but was back running within six weeks of the operation. Keeping away from the gym, he focused on more GAA-orientated exercises with physio O'Connor: jumping, landing, sprinting, side-to-side leaps, bouncing and jerking. It worked. With Stradbally faring so well in the Waterford football championship there was a temptation to hop back upon the merry-go-round before Christmas but he decided to stay put. Four months he spent on his own.

'I knew if I came back I would only end up doing more damage,' he admits. 'I wasn't ready for action even though I would have given anything to get back out there. I was playing with a fantastic club and it's professional there – it was a major blow missing all that. But the muscle in my thigh went to jelly after the operation and for stability I needed to replicate actions that happen in a game. People get fed up of hearing about it now and I'm fed up talking about it as well.'

His colleagues can't wait to get him back in tow, and in interviews Kiely regularly name-checks him. Thanks to this media exposure outsiders now have this impression of a decorated warrior waiting impatiently on the sidelines desperate to get back into battle and lead his troops into the Promised Land.

'That's Jackson,' Power chuckles heartily at the depiction. 'He will always blow things up. He has me made out to be Jesus Christ Superstar since I've been injured and the irony is that I was playing total shite when I did the knee against Carlow in the first place. But that's his way,' he laughs. 'He'll always instil confidence.'

For Power, the frustration of trying to make a breakthrough under Kiely was harder than for most. Recognised as one of their best-ever footballers, he essentially sacrificed two seasons of his career warming his ass on the bench for the hurlers. It was 2005 when he got the call from Justin McCarthy to dine with the great and good. He says he had no hesitation in joining the top table.

'There would be plenty of hurlers here with way more skill than me,' he admits, 'but at the same time I felt I had a role to play. I felt I would bring a bit of steel to the backs and I thought that was badly needed, to be honest.'

The dream, however, quickly whizzed by, like the flash of a firefly in the light.

'Justin had his 17 players and the rest of us were up at the other end of the pitch. I knew pretty quickly that I wasn't going to make the team, but you always have a glimmer of hope at the same time. So I spent the whole season there. He said I wasn't too far away from the team but I was playing football too and a few weeks into June I asked him if I was going to be used because the footballers were playing Offaly in the qualifiers and they badly needed me.

'He reassured me that I was close to his starting 15 against Offaly but yet I was left on the bench for the entire game. Meanwhile, the footballers lost by a goal to Louth in their qualifier. One goal. That really pissed me off – I felt I could have helped them. The hurlers rolled on to Croker and Cork beat us in the 2005 semi-final and still looking to make a break, a year later I went back in and rejoined the panel again. Like the four lads are probably doing now, I said I'd give it the league and see how it goes.

'With Justin you had to serve an apprenticeship and stay on the bench for a year anyway,' he reflects. 'It was pathetic. We travelled to Down in the 2006 league. They had just got over some sort of bust-up and we were winning by 15 points when Eoin Murphy got injured and came off. My chance, I thought. But no.

'Someone else got injured and they put Eoin back on again. Talk about insulting a lad. The footballers were back onto me a day later looking to know how much longer I'd sit on the bench and I knew my time with the hurlers was up. I did all I could – went through the army camp training in Kildare, made every training session and yet I didn't even get one minute of league action. I always kept the football channel open, though, and back I went. Thank God.'

Still, having spent two seasons soaring with the eagles, even though he never got a chance to fully spread his wings, it was a nice change from flapping in the wetlands of lower-division football.

'Well, there's a huge difference between both camps,' he says. 'The money that football brings in is non-existent for a start so they get little back. I wouldn't have blamed lads for trying the hurling and giving football a break for a while. At one stage things were utterly terrible for football in this county; we trained in the Dungarvan showgrounds some nights, where the lights were shite and there were floods on the pitch. Afterwards you'd get a few sandwiches in the dressing room. That's only a few years ago.

'Then Jackson came in and didn't draw a line in the sand – you could play both codes. He didn't go chasing any player and in turn lads ended up going with him. He supported me through the injury – I didn't hear too much from others and as for the insurance money, well you're on your own really. I was working for myself and got the operation done through my own VHI. I got fast-tracked through a clinic.

'People hear all this, but it goes in one ear and out the other,' he says. 'The main thing is that we're being treated better now and we're getting better results. That's down to the manager. Maybe not everyone wants to see that progress, though.

'The county board are not putting a whole lot into football and so you couldn't blame lads for going with the hurlers. We know we might never play in Croke Park whereas the hurlers are in and around the big time every week. Bar we draw Dublin in the football qualifiers we might never get to Croker. That would be the dream, I've never played there.'

Nonetheless, if they can keep the show on the road there is hope that someday their old team bus might snail up the N9 into Dublin City and edge over towards Jones' Road.

'Stranger things have happened, I suppose,' Power shrugs. 'You never can tell. A bit of luck would help. Last year [2008] the injuries killed us,' he says. 'By the time the championship came around we had nothing left. The league was our best league ever and it was a shame we didn't make it.

'This year our backs are fantastic, we're good in midfield but we're lacking in the forwards. I was hoping Shane Walsh would be the difference up front. Hopefully we'll get Patrick and John back. But with Gary gone we've no target man or free-taker. The young lads will have to find their feet and please God they will. Michael O'Gorman and Seán O'Hare are the lads to bring it forward now.'

41

Ogle – the GPA Rep

——•——

TRAINING is over for the morning but they're told to be back again tomorrow. Same time, same place. With two weeks to go to the start of the national league the players decide to hold a meeting.

Paul Ogle, their GPA representative, takes the floor. He teaches in the city's De La Salle College and has an immediate hold on the 18 footballers who hang around. There are a number of items on the agenda and he steers them impressively through each one.

Meals? 'Terrible' seems to be the general reaction from the squad. They are looked after well enough when they eat in Lawlor's Hotel but the meals-on-wheels unit that visits them after training and specialises in plates of chicken curry and rice –and sometimes, for a change, rice and chicken curry – isn't going down too well.

'It's pure slop sometimes,' moans one player, 'and seemingly it costs €8 a plate. But the hurlers can go to the Ramada Hotel after training and get whatever they want. We're no different from them. Why can't we have what they have?'

Others add their voices to a chorus of agreement. The consensus, it's fair to say, is that Gordon Ramsey is safe enough for the time being.

'Right,' Ogle nods, 'I'll get onto it straight away.'

Training. No problems here. Ogle himself starts the ball rolling.

'I have to say it's more varied this year and in fairness to Jackson, bringing Paul on board has been a great addition,' he says. 'He's working very well with Mick too, which is great. What do ye think?'

There's a hum of approval from the floor. Training is going well. The only problem is there aren't enough bodies on the field. Among the points made is that the players would like to work more on tactical preparation.

But at this stage, numbers, or the lack of, are really getting to Ahearne and he's keen to have his say. He has great faith in the adage that light is the task where many share the toil and he's sick to the teeth of seeing only the same old faces day in, day out.

'It's not good enough, lads – it's impossible to do work on tactics or anything else if there are only 12 or so there,' he points out.

It's noted that even fewer are buying into the weights training. So far, only one player on the team has a 100 per cent record of making every session and that's Ogle. He tosses out the idea of new players being brought in to supplement the squad. The players reckon they know who is good enough to ask in and propose that they draw up a list for management to consider. The notion of not being able to propose a club colleague is also put forward. And Ogle warns his teammates not to name-check a footballer, however good he is, if they cannot vouch that he will put in the effort. He scribbles a note in his jotter and adds it to the to-do list.

GPA player grants. They're all safely in the kitty by now. They were cut by eight per cent or so and with the economy floundering it could be the last they ever see of them. But there is general acceptance that because the cuts are across the board, encompassing all sports, they're fine with whatever happens. The money is welcome, but it's not the reason they do this. Scarcely 20 seconds are devoted to this topic.

The whereabouts of the €35,000 they themselves raised two years ago gets a bit more attention. The players argue that they devoted massive time and energy to collecting that money but never got as much as a team holiday out of it. They would like further information as to why they never benefited from raising that sum.

Sponsorship. There are issues but even though it's only January, it's probably too late to do anything about them. They reckon they should be getting more in overall terms. Lawlor's Hotel have been looking after them for a while but the squad is demanding more protein drinks and a few more perks besides. They formulate a request that the energy drink 'Revive' be provided at the end of every session. The drink includes all the necessary nutrients and is made by Glanbia, the sponsors of the hurling team.

Ogle reckons getting a supply of that should be no problem but points out that the players' hands are tied with regard to overall sponsorship deals.

He reveals he had been hopeful of securing a €30,000 sponsorship deal with John West (of salmon fame) in the recent past but it came to nothing.

'Thank God for that,' exclaims Wayne Hennessy, known as 'The Bomber'. 'Jaysus, we're bad enough as it is, but can you imagine us leaving training every Tuesday and Thursday with a big salmon in our hands or wearing the head of an oul fish on our jerseys?'

Laughter all round. On that note, the chairman points out that all gear requests have been made and the necessary kit should be with the players shortly: 'The order is gone into Azurri, and there's no problem there.'

Training facilities? They get the thumbs-up. Once they can kick a ball under lights they are not complaining.

The players are asked if there is any other business but Ogle barely gets a reply. There's a stampede out the door and the players pile into their cars and hit the road like hares on speed. The Munster Rugby team are in action against Montauban in a Heineken Cup lunchtime kick-off. That might explain the exodus.

'Adios,' Ogle waves to his colleagues. The meeting has lasted 20 minutes in total but it's enough to keep everyone focused – and keeping communication channels open between players and management helps prevent any minor issue from becoming a major crisis.

This team may be walking slowly but they're not going backwards. Onward and upward.

Spinning the Yarn

28 January, Piltown, County Kilkenny

THESE are worrying times of trauma and national crisis. The airwaves groan with the demise of the economy. Hundreds of jobs are disappearing daily. Brian Cowen addresses the first sitting of the Dáil since Christmas to tell the country to back off – he knows what he's doing. That's more or less what Diarmuid McMurrough said when he invited the Normans to Ireland.

But if our great leader thinks he's having it tough he should sit down and have a chat with Jackson.

There are just 10 days before the start of the national league when an interview with the Waterford manager headed 'Nightmare before February' hits the national press and various GAA websites. The 2010 Book of Estimates would make better reading and the piece suggests the team is on the verge of implosion.

For once, the poor old writer cannot be blamed for hyping up this crisis; Jackson has thrown the kitchen sink at his interviewer with a frank and truly desolate assessment of where he and the team stand.

'The scenario for Waterford football at present is catastrophic,' he groans. 'For our first game in the league, we will be without nine of last season's championship starting side. The whole thing is like a nightmare.'

Of course, this is all spin. He has already told the team to ignore most of what he says in the media for the year ahead. He has also advised them not to read too much into what others write about them either. 'One man's opinion,' he says. 'Don't fall for it.'

Surely, though, having such a negative article appear in several national newspapers will seep through to the team, even if it is an accurate summation of where the team is at. 'Ah look,' he says indignantly, 'I'm only trying to play down the thing; sure all we want to do is lower expectations and catch Wicklow on the hop.'

'Come here, the players know Jackson well enough by now,' Tom Condon chips in. 'They all know the story. If we can get an advantage by having teams think we're a write-off then we'll do it.' Both men then proceed to wheeze hearty chuckles at the contents of the article.

'Ah, sure there are enough managers giving the party line,' Kiely shrugs. 'At least I'm giving the reporters something interesting.'

In truth, they're in grand old form; tonight, in a one-sided challenge match against WIT, they land their third win from four games. Condon, though, says there's nothing to get excited about – an under-14 team would

45

have provided sterner opposition than the college lads. Nevertheless, there were highlights. They employed the tactic of bringing an extra man back into defence. They also played three midfielders. Crucially, they appear to have found a full-forward; Maurice O'Gorman was a revelation, scoring 2-4 and looking highly impressive in the 4-14 to 1-5 win.

But – and there's always a but in these parts – Kiely's plans have received yet another dent with the news that their tight-marking young corner-back Shane Lannon, a tigerish and speedy defender and a carpenter by trade, is struggling for work and has decided to head for Australia. He becomes another statistic, the latest to withdraw from the panel.

Employment opportunites had dried up for the 21-year-old in recent months and he had been mulling over the prospect of starting anew Down Under. When two of his friends made the move, he booked a flight and was headed to join his pals in Sydney.

He'll be a loss; it was his second season on the panel and there was a natural progression involved. In the McGrath Cup semi-final against UL, Lannon marked Enda Varley and though the elusive corner-forward was the college's best player on the day, the young defender's potential was there to see, especially under the dropping ball.

It's another player gone, but Lannon had no choice.

'Work is scarce in my field and it's getting scarcer,' he explained before leaving.

'There's not a whole lot happening jobwise and there won't be either for a few years by the looks of things. I had been thinking of moving for a while and then the friends said they were off. That really made my mind up. I told Paul McLoughlin at training the other night and he said he'd tell the rest of the management for me, so I haven't actually been speaking to Jackson or anyone yet. I suppose if I was in a county where we had a better chance of doing something I might have had second thoughts about leaving the country.

'But even as it is, I'll be missing playing for my club Stradbally too. I suppose I'm just frustrated at the moment. I seem to be injured all the time and with the work situation being as bad as it is now, this is the time to move. I'm sure I'll be back in the future. My sister is getting married during the year and I'll be back for that anyway. I'll just see how it goes. There are plenty of Irish people over in Sydney and we're already sorted with a club there so I'll keep fit.

'I just hope the lads do well in Division 4. I think they have a chance of getting promotion but they badly need the Hurneys to come back. Without them, I don't think they'll do it.'

Emigration is a nationwide blight but the modern-day flight of the sporting earls is mostly confined to weaker counties. There would be no chance, for instance, of Kerry letting Colm Cooper go abroad to earn a crust; a job would be found somewhere. A Waterford footballer, however, holds little clout.

As with the others, Kiely remains philosophical about the latest departure and says he won't be chasing anyone. Again, he's focused on who he has. With Maurice O'Gorman shaping up nicely, the selectors have decided to build the attack around him. This weekend they're going to use only four forwards in a challenge match against the Munster club champions, Dromcollogher-Broadford, and crowd their defence. They might find it hard to score, but it will be just as hard to score against them.

All week long they've been working on this tactic in training and the challenge match against the Limerick club side in Garryspillane will be their last chance to use the move before the Wicklow game.

Meanwhile, Kiely has considered the players' requests to bring some new faces in but has other ideas.

'Look, we're around for years, but some of the players are only in a little while. The truth is that in a county like this you only need a small panel with everyone guaranteed a bit of game time and everyone pushing each other. I've found that if I carry a 30-man panel there's a lot of bitching and it usually comes from lads who don't have much of a hope of a game. I'm carrying 24 lads and that's it. I have the best players in the county in with me – I'm not going looking for others.'

He's not for turning.

* * *

31 January, Garryspillane, County Limerick

MICK O'Loughlin texts the squad to confirm that the game against Dromcollogher-Broadford, the All-Ireland club hopefuls, is going ahead despite a downpour that has Clonmel flooded. With villages like Ardfinnan under water, O'Loughlin has pin-pointed alternative routes for the team to navigate.

The game is down for 2.30 p.m. and 10 minutes beforehand Dromcollogher are out on the field, warming up and undergoing some intense drills. Their opposition, however, are still careering around the roads and bohreens of County Limerick, trying to find the pitch. It's nicely sandwiched between Limerick City, Tipperary Town and Mitchelstown and the journey takes some plotting. Then, just at throw-in time, a convoy of cars pulls up – the Waterford team has arrived.

As they file in, most of the chat is about the previous night's sit-in protest by 500 Waterford Crystal workers after being told their jobs were gone. None of the team works there but most have family members or relations involved. It's not a good time.

This is where football can help – a chance to get away from it all for a little while. Today, there are 22 players ready and waiting. Comeback kids Shane Briggs and Ger Power are present too, both of them reaching the end of the cruciate recovery timetable and it gives the rest a boost to see them near full flow again.

Inside the dressing room, Kiely lays it on the line.

'These lads are a good team,' he states. 'They beat Nemo Rangers in the club championship and they have three or four Limerick senior players and another eight or nine who have played intercounty football. So be ready for them. But fuck it, lads, you're an intercounty team so play with confidence. Stick your chests out and play with a bit of swagger. We're using Thomas O'Gorman as a sweeper today and we'll have four forwards. Paul, over to you.'

Paul McLoughlin addresses them succinctly. 'You're the county team, play with pride. There will be two men inside the 14-yard-line at all times so low diagonal balls into them. You're allowed only three seconds on the ball, after that it moves on. We defend en masse and break together. A bit of fucking pride, lads,' he says as he moves away.

Kiely chips back in. 'Everyone will get a run. We're looking at this game to pick a team for Wicklow next Saturday. That's our big one but show me today that ye want to play.'

As they file out of the dressing room, selector Ger Power encourages them individually by chanting the mantra 'Wicklow next Saturday' as they pass.

Both teams must have feared playing in a bog but Garryspillane's pitch is in beautiful condition, a real testament to the €200,000 spent on draining it. It allows for decent, flowing football and while both teams play a little negatively, the game does move from end to end.

At half-time the club side lead by a point, but Waterford have had two goal chances saved by the Limerick side's keeper. Wayne Hennessy is deployed as a running wing-back and performs his role to good effect. Eddie Rockett is another lethal attacking force from centre-back. Thomas O'Gorman is like a flycatcher on the edge of his square, gobbling up anything that comes his way.

It's a game Waterford desperately want to win; their former coach Ned English is training Dromcollogher and in addition they don't want to lose to a club side. A raft of changes are made – six players coming off during the second half – and the new recruits have their shooting boots on. They win 0-15 to 0-14 and are happy enough.

Inside, Jackson congratulates his men and directs their focus to the following weekend. There are still plenty of problems. Michael O'Gorman went over on an ankle in the warm-up and damaged it. They couldn't land a free for love nor money. In front of the posts they tend to delay before shooting, allowing opponents to close them down. Little wonder that management has drafted in Colin Kenny from Louth, a forwards and kicking coach, to spend the following day with them. Training is scheduled for noon tomorrow; the players will be coached in off-the-ball running, and three or four will be held back to practise free-taking. With Hurney absent, they have no natural marksman in their ranks. And in Division 4 that's a potential killer.

One by one, they head for home. Tonight, Dublin open the national league with a game against Tyrone in front of 80,000 people in Croke Park. It will be bright and brash and spectacular as the GAA marks its 125th anniversary with €500,000 worth of crackling fireworks and dazzling lights. U2's Larry Mullen has been drafted in to choreograph the show.

But right here, in the hairy armpit of Limerick, after 16 training sessions, five bouts of weights training and four wins out of five matches, January, the month of the empty pocket in Ireland, draws to a close for the Waterford footballers. They may be more brass band than U2 and may exist a million miles away from Croke Park but without them the GAA would not be rejoicing in this latest milestone.

One guy who epitomises their effort is Liam Lawlor. Shortly after the final whistle he leaves Limerick for Shannon Airport. Each week he travels to and from university in Scotland to play football for his county. The rewards are few and far between but it doesn't cost him a second thought.

He believes in what he's doing – that one day the dream will come true.

Chapter 4
The Flying Scotsman (Liam Lawlor's Story)

The Edinburgh Engineer

6 February, Edinburgh

I DON'T have that long left here now so I may as well enjoy the last of it. I'll be sad to leave, I suppose. It's like a second home.

I'm studying at the Napier University, already been here two years and I've had the time of my life. There was never any question of longing for Waterford or getting homesick, but then again when you've half of Ireland over here it helps. Around 19 lads from my class in Waterford IT came over and I'm living with four of them. There are Scottish locals walking around here with Irish accents with so many Paddies about.

The plan? Work hard and walk away with an Honours Degree in Civil Engineering. That would be nice to stick on the wall anyway. Put it like this; after three years in WIT and two here, I'd better have something to show the parents.

We live in an area of Edinburgh called Polworth, all residential and built up, a real student paradise. It's close to the college and fairly central to town. It's fine. The digs cost about £300 a month. Not too bad. Overall, I'm getting away lightly; my course fees are paid for by some fund called the PSAS, the Postgraduate Students Allowances Scheme. Now, I don't know the people who run this group but I think I'll send them a Christmas card. They're after saving me about £5,000 in course fees and that's a huge whack of money that I wouldn't have had.

I have few regrets about my time here but there are one or two things I might have done differently.

For a start, I didn't get to know too many Scottish people and maybe that was silly. You normally make friends with the locals but with so many here from Ireland there was never really a need.

And since the start of the New Year I've only actually stayed here for two weekends. That doesn't particularly help the whole cultural integration process either. Don't get me wrong – I have plenty of craic during the week with the lads but the social intensity goes up another level at the weekends, when I'm hardly ever around.

Why? The same reason that I can't get a part-time job in Edinburgh, the same reason that I'm over and back on a Ryanair flight the whole time. Gaelic football.

This is my third year playing senior for Waterford and while the rest of my gang in Scotland give me a right slagging for trekking over and back I don't mind. No one is forcing me.

At the moment I'm getting ready to go back for the Wicklow game and my routine is pretty straightforward. I'd normally fly out from Edinburgh Airport at 10.55 on a Saturday morning and arrive in Shannon at 11.45. The flight is only 50 minutes, so you can nod off on the way over and be fresh enough when you arrive. The mother and father would normally be waiting for me and from the airport I'd usually be ferried to some match or other. My brother, Shane, is studying in UL so if I was in at any half-decent hour he'd often wait for me.

We live outside Clonmel – the right side of the border, mind – and that's an hour and 45 minutes of a spin from Shannon, but when you take that route so often, you don't even notice it.

I've had a few close calls. I went from Edinburgh to Cardiff to watch the Heineken Cup final last year. The plan was simple; fly down to Bristol and hire a car. Of course there's all this fine print and when I reach Bristol they wouldn't give me a car because I was only 22. I had to get two trains, a bus and a taxi to fly back to Shannon Airport the next morning. We were playing a championship game against Clare. I arrived in a few hours before the game and we were pure shite on the same day.

Earlier in the season, I came back from Scotland and we left Dungarvan to play Antrim in Casement Park. We went the evening before the match and planned to stay in Dundalk. Sure we were travelling an hour and still hadn't gone past Clonmel with so many lads getting picked up all over the place. And after four hours of travelling the bus driver decided enough was enough. He pulled in somewhere in Dublin. He had a Tacograph or something and wasn't allowed drive any further. Most lads would plough on but not this lad. He insisted on taking a break and sure we were stuck on the bloody bus for another hour and a half. We were starving. I think we went through a box of Mars bars. Eventually we reached Dundalk that night. And we went out and beat Antrim the next day. That's Waterford football for ya, the minute we're expected to do something we go the opposite way. And then when the odds are stacked against us we usually come out fighting.

Because I play hurling as well, there's always something on at the weekends – little wonder that I've hardly been in Edinburgh all year. Take the Christmas just gone: we reached the Waterford football final, which wasn't played until the last week of December. A shambles. Some torture going over and back for that. I had an exam on the Saturday, flew home for the final on Sunday – we beat Ballinacourty by four points – and then flew back to Edinburgh for another exam on the Tuesday.

And people say students have it easy.

Ah sure we do, I suppose. It's a different world really. The boys were out on the town last night and could get a bottle of beer for £1. Where else would you get it? It's as cheap as chips over here. Maybe I should go back for another course.

Still, when you're playing sport to any high level you try to minimise the socialising. I try hard to keep fit myself but I wouldn't be at the same level as the rest of the team – they're definitely a good notch above. I tip away in the gym and we actually have a good GAA club in college so I'm always ticking over. That's something, at least.

We won the British Universities hurling championship last year and got to compete in the third tier of the Fitzgibbon Cup – the Fergal Maher Cup they call it. We played GMIT Letterfrack in the final and won – a huge result for us, the first time a British team ever got that far.

The final was played on the same day as the Fitzgibbon Cup and the Ryan Cup. We were the third-choice fare and there was no one around to watch but to us it was a massive thing. It always means more when you're away from home.

So I'm kept going. The key to surviving with a county team is doing individual training sessions but I'd be pretty laid-back and it's hard to push yourself hard when you're on your own.

Along Came Davy Fitz

If I was still playing hurling with Waterford I would have no choice.

I was first called into the county hurling team at 18. I thought it was all going to unfold from there. I actually played five league games in my first season and thought I was onto a winner. But sad to say, that was about the peak of it. I got two games when I was 19, two games when I was 20 and for the year of my 21st birthday I got no game at all.

Justin McCarthy called me up but I think he was a difficult person to figure out – a great coach, but very old-fashioned – and after a few years I wasn't even featuring anymore, only on the fringes of the squad.

There was the time when my first cousin was getting married. We were after getting slaughtered in a league match and it was before the championship match against Clare, which we ended up winning by a cricket score. In between we had a challenge match against Offaly but it fell the same day as my cousin's wedding. Obviously I wanted to go to the wedding and told the management of my plans. But I was told not to attend, that I was being considered for the Offaly game.

The first thing I did was ring the cousin and explain the circumstances. But sure I went along to the match and spent the whole 80 minutes, four quarters of 20, looking on from the bench. Never even came near getting a run. I think Justin and I had sort of a personality clash because I couldn't even get a bit of action in a challenge game at the end.

Then Davy Fitz took over. Straight away he called me into his squad. Gary Hurney got the nod too. But I had exams at the time and was two weeks late linking up. By then Davy was after running the rule over most of the lads and had his new squad – which was fair enough. I ended up playing for the intermediate hurlers in the championship but I was part of the travelling panel for the All-Ireland senior final against Kilkenny last year. Jesus, it was a different world. We were staying in five star hotels, the likes of Dromoland Castle and that and any demand we had was met. The hurlers are the Hollywood story around here and fair enough. I was watching them in the Munster championship last year and they must have hit €300 worth of sliothars into the crowd. Not a word said to them by the county board. Christ, if we lost an oul football in the ditches in Dungarvan there would be torches and lamps produced for us until we found it.

I'm turning 24 in June and didn't get the nod from the senior hurlers at all this year so that's basically that for my intercounty career. It means I can focus on the footballers and play a bit of intermediate hurling along the way, I suppose. With the club and the college commitments, that's more than enough.

I won't tell you a lie, the first Waterford football game I was ever at was the first one I played in – the 2006 league opener against Wicklow. Over the years when we were growing up they were complete shite and there never was much of a reason to watch them. That might sound harsh but that's the way it was. You would support the hurlers because they were nearly always at a high level but sure the footballers were always in Division 4. There was just no point going to their games.

In many ways, you'd nearly be looking down on them.

The Nire is my club and along with our rivals Stradbally and Ballinacourty we'd all be pretty strong outfits. We wouldn't fear playing anyone in Ireland because we're used to winning. We'd think nothing of going down to play Nemo Rangers and beating them.

But with the county footballers, there was always this losing mentality which has taken so long to get rid of – although we're making progress on that score.

When I came in I saw that it was definitely a psychological thing – we'd be motoring well in games but then we'd concede a few scores and would cave in once pressure was put on.

And it's only now I can say what respect I have for the likes of Budgie, Paul Ogle and Mick Ahearne. Jesus, they've gone through some horrific times.

I only came in at the tail-end of it. In my first season we would sit down, target a few counties and hope to beat them. In year two we might head up to Sligo or Cavan and catch them on the hop. They were realistic goals, but we wanted more.

The Jackson Way

I remember the first time I met Jackson. He called me up but I was injured and sat out the first few training sessions. We were in Fraher Field one afternoon and training was in full swing but there was no sign of Jackson at all. Next thing he walks in with the biggest smile on his face and starts patting us all on the backs.

'Jesus, there's a happy man,' one of the boys said to him.

'Why wouldn't I be ?' he replied. 'Got a double at 7/1.'

He was down in the bookies and came back with an oul envelope bulging with cash. Sure he was as happy as Larry going onto that field. That's my first memory of the man.

He's done a lot for us; these days we look at every team in Division 4 and feel we can give them all a run.

My turning point was the game against Offaly last year; they were hammering teams all around them but up we went, trailed by a point at the break and lost by the same margin in the end. We should have got a result but it showed us there was no need to fear anyone. After that we won three league games on the trot, games that I missed because of exams.

But when I came back it was like walking into a different camp; the confidence had soared and there was a totally different outlook; the lads were winning and suddenly everyone was enjoying the whole thing. In the past we were losing week after week, confidence was low and players were leaving steadily.

Now our camp is a mighty solid one. There are no divisions between the selectors and players – we're all in it together. We're deadly serious about it but we have a laugh at the same time. I love it when Jackson drives into training with the oul John Denver hat on him.

There's still people talking about the time he wore the Glasgow Rangers jersey; sure I'd say he didn't have a notion what he was wearing. But that's the sort of craic we have. We also love reading the doom-and-gloom stories that Jackson often sends out to the media, probably to try and pull the wool over people's eyes.

Everyone looks out for each other. I pay for my own flights home and when I show the backroom boys the receipts, they reimburse me. It means I can keep up this lark.

I respect the management and think they have a bit of time for me too. I was always a forward but they're starting to play me as a link-man between the full-back and half-back lines. I enjoy that. I get on the ball a lot more; it brings me right into the game and hopefully it gives the team a bit of a tactical edge too.

We're all thinking the same thing this year; it would be some reward for all the hard work to get out of the bottom division, whatever about the championship. I have my goals set – an Honours Degree and promotion would do me nicely, thanks very much.

I'd be motivated like that, but at the same time I would keep it to myself. I don't agree with this thing of a sheet being passed around the dressing room at the start of every year and the players being asked what their personal goals are and what the aim for the team is. That's shite as far as I'm concerned. I did all that in the past and found I was writing the same old stuff year in, year out. I'm not one for sitting down and doing that anymore. I think every year should be treated differently because no two things are the same from season to season.

I can't look too far ahead. Where would you be going setting public targets for yourself when you have exams and that? I'd be taking it week by week. One injury and the whole thing could go up in smoke for you.

For now, I'll continue to fly over and back but I have a thesis to get done before April as well. After that, we have a big group project to submit. Then we're done and dusted.

It's gas – there were hundreds of civil engineering jobs out there when we started out in college and now, five years later when we've done our bit, there are no jobs at all – either in Scotland or back home. You'd have to go to Alaska, Dubai or somewhere to get a bit of work in that field. I couldn't see Jackson flying me back from there.

People will say I was nuts, coming over and back the whole time, but sure it was all I wanted to do. After seeing the passion the rest of the boys have for the team you get a right taste for it yourself.

And then sense goes out the window. Your whole week revolves around Saturday or Sunday.

And putting on that jersey.

Chapter 5
Micko and The Cats

The Battle of Aughrim

7 January, Aughrim, County Wicklow.
National Football League (NFL) Round 1

The dressing room fizzes with adrenalin and the players, not long off the field, are already hopping about, shuffling anxiously from foot to foot, desperate to get back out.

It's half-time in Waterford's first league match of the year and they lead Wicklow, their bogey team of recent years, by 1-4 to 0-4. The home crowd at Aughrim can't believe it, but for the past 30 minutes their side has been played off the pitch by Kiely's men.

Eddie Rockett can't handle the silence anymore.

Bursting to cajole his colleagues he jumps off his seat and lays it on the line: 'This is the first time we've ever led at half-time against this crowd and I'll tell you one thing, lads, we're not going to be beaten by them today. I'm fucking sick of it, lads, every year warming down on the field, disappointed, and them trotting off the pitch delighted after beating us again. That's not happening today.'

Silence once more, but only for a few seconds – there's way too much nervous energy in the room for the stillness to prevail.

A result here against the odds and their crusade for promotion takes on a new impetus. Every player knows the importance of coming away with something.

'Just keep doing what we're doing,' Ahearne advises in that calm way of his. 'Keep making the runs, laying the ball off quickly and supporting each other. Everything else will fall into place.'

By now, all the players are up on their feet, dancing with pent-up energy, eager to get back out to war. Paul McLoughlin winces at their impatience. 'Lads, will ye sit down – ye have another eight minutes before we go back out. Just relax and breathe it out.'

He drifts out of the dressing room to confer with the rest of the management team. You can tell he's almost as excited as the players, and though he dare not let them know it, the look on his face speaks volumes.

It's the turn of the selector Ger Power to have a say. 'You have them rattled, you're fitter and our game-plan is better,' he adds. 'We are well on top, but I'd ask you not to even look at the scoreboard, just keep going through the plays and it will happen for us.'

The scoreboard is certainly reassuring. Just last year Wicklow beat Kildare in the Leinster championship and the season before they came out on top after three epic battles with Louth. When their championship hopes finally ended, they dropped back to the Tommy Murphy Cup, Gaelic football's 'B' competition, which they won. Under Mick O'Dwyer, that wise old firebrand, they are a team reborn, capable of taking on the big hitters and causing a shock.

Today, though, Micko's men are being run ragged. Mervyn Travers, their goalkeeper, has already made three top-drawer saves from Liam Ó Líonáin – saves that would illuminate any stage. They are having their own personal duel, like gunslingers going head to head in a sleepy town.

Although he's on fire, Ó Líonáin takes the wrong option more than once in front of the posts and simple chances go a-begging. With every goal attempt fluffed, those on the Waterford sideline cringe and plead with him to fist the next chance over the bar. Eventually he gets the better of his nemesis and the resultant goal leaves them in pole position.

Still, the magnitude of it all might just affect them; that's the worry. They've been in the doldrums so long they dare not dream of one day escaping.

Sensing the tension, Kiely walks in and offers this summary.

'Last year we watched our country beat Australia in the International Rules. Leighton Glynn was one of Ireland's best players but today we have young Conor McGrath on him, a slip of a lad in his first-ever league game, and he has him wrapped up. Glynn got away to make one run during the first half but young Conor got back and dispossessed him.

'Lads, what have ye got to be afraid of? Nothing. I have nothing against Wicklow. I respect them, but I'm sick of them – they're the only team in this division that I haven't beaten and I want that rectified today'

As they gulp down Club Energise and chew bananas, the players are issued with final instructions. 'Three seconds on the ball, pass, run and pass again. The rest will look after itself,' McLoughlin yells.
And with that it's out into the light again.

Micko looks a little perplexed as he strolls back out to the sideline, programme rolled up as usual in his right hand. Before the game he had felt secure enough to rest two of his Under-21 stars, Ciaran Walsh and Darren Hayden. The pair are due to play a Leinster championship fixture the following day but now they're on the field for the second half. Having drawn with Antrim last week, Micko badly needs his full-strength team to dig out a win here.

From the restart it's clear his legendary motivational powers have not waned over the years. Wicklow post three quickfire points before a shellshocked Waterford regain composure and surge ahead again. The pendulum swings wildly back and forth as the game unfolds.

Wicklow go two points up once more as full-time looms. It looks like another sob story for Kiely's men. But wait – from deep in defence they kickstart yet another attack and in a series of quick passes the ball is worked upfield. It reaches Cillian O'Keeffe, who shifts it like a hot potato to Ó Líonáin – who hammers a goal to put them a point up.

Almost immediately Wicklow draw level again. This is frantic stuff.

In a nerve-racking finale Brian Wall and Maurice O'Gorman miss golden chances to win the game, both somehow shooting wide from 20 yards out. The final whistle sounds. It's 0-15 to 2-9, a draw. The Waterford players don't know whether to laugh or cry.

Wicklow's captain, Glynn, is feeling exactly the same emotions.

'That's the first time we haven't managed to beat them in ages,' he says, gasping for breath. 'They were bloody hard to play against but sure we could have won just as easily. The one thing I'll say is that every time one of them made a run there was a support sprinter on each side. No team in this division could handle that. Now, we missed a load of chances but they were back at us every time. They're fitter this year than before and play to more of a tactical plan as well.

'We rested a few of the younger lads, I suppose, but there are no excuses. Waterford deserved a point and maybe even to win if I'm being honest. They're big lads, well-drilled, but I knew beforehand that we wouldn't walk over them and I told our boys that. Only for Mervyn we were in right trouble, he made three or four great saves. Still, I thought we had them at the end although they missed two chances at the death. It was that type of game.'

Warm plaudits, but Glynn should see the Waterford dressing room. It's like a morgue; heads are down and the mood is one of gloom, a complete contrast to the half-time scenes.

Except for 10 or 15 minutes the other side of the break they'd had squatters' rights in the Wicklow half and had been by far the better team.

Micko knows that too. Outside he tells the reporters Kiely's team are definitely fit. Respect from a legend like O'Dwyer should boost the Waterford players but instead it's as if they've lost a Munster final. The heavy silence is punctuated only by the gush of water spitting off the tiles in the shower-room. No one speaks.

'It's as though we've lost,' Kiely explains in the treatment room next door. 'That's how far we've come over the years. Players are angry with themselves for not clinching the win we deserved and that is good. They've put in a lot of work and while everyone will expect us to beat Kilkenny next weekend we will be taking nothing for granted.

'We have two away games, against Clare and London, to follow that and if we can get something from those we'll be in a good position to challenge for promotion with home games against Leitrim, Carlow and Antrim to follow. A lot of those teams are going to take points off each other so the race is wide open. We have as good a chance as any of them.'

Back to the dressing room moments after the match, everyone packs up and boards the bus home. They stop on the road back to eat dinner and watch Ireland take on France in the Six Nations at Croke Park. Declan Kidney's men play brilliant rugby and secure a famous win. It helps lift the mood. By the time they reach Dungarvan that evening, the Waterford players are ready to consider the positives of a point in Aughrim.

It's more than they have managed in many a year.

Grub and Gear

9 February, Piltown, County Kilkenny

THE following Monday night the team regroup at their regular training base and there's little or no mention of the Wicklow game. Sport is like that; you quickly move on, scarcely look back.

Numbers are good tonight in this Kilkenny venue; there was no pitch with floodlights available in Waterford – just imagine. There are 24 players togged out and soon they are into a series of gut-wrenching strides and dashes. By the end of the night, some of the players estimate they have sprinted more than four kilometres. Full of gusto, they kicked off with

300-metre darts and, cutting 50 metres off each run, worked right back to a 40-metre sprint before building it back up all over again.

Seven times they repeated the same block of exercises. All the way through they were monitored. By the end of the session their zest had long since disappeared into the darkened skies. They were heaving.

But further tests awaited them. The next target was a 100-metre sprint in 30 seconds. Then they had to beat that time in their next run. Not Usain Bolt territory, but try doing it when your legs are weaker than a newborn foal's and your pulse is up around 200.

When the hardship came to an end they were taken through another coaching module by McLoughlin. Footballs fizzed around the field and one by one the players were taken aside and reminded of their duties. Targets were set. McLoughlin told them he wanted more scores from the half-back line. And right through the team he issued challenges.

The players are now tactically aware of their roles.

Left half-back Paul Ogle gulps down water while taking a breather. He's clearly enjoying the increased tempo and fruits of McLoughlin's wisdom.

'I've been told to be a flanker, a link-man, and to serve up and down the field,' he reveals. 'I'll have a freedom I didn't have years ago. I remember in 2005, before we played Kerry in the championship, I was pulled aside and told to 'man mark Paul Galvin'.

'Simple as that. I tried my best and actually didn't do too bad but I didn't contribute one thing to the team. When I came in off the field all I had was this negative feeling. I was not in a very constructive state of mind. Whereas these days I'm being told to burst forward and get a point a game. It's bloody refreshing, to be honest.'

He goes back for the final stint and they wind the session down. Although there's still a definite residue of regret following the Wicklow game, tonight has gone a long way toward putting a sheen back on the surface. By the time they pack up and head homeward, the glass is most definitely half-full again.

'We were disgusted at leaving it behind us,' Ogle comments. 'We had so many goal chances it was hard to stomach. But even though I'm still pissed off, it's a point more than we got off them last year and, more importantly, I'm delighted they only got a point – one more slip-up and they could be out of the promotion race. Maybe down the road we might see the Wicklow game as a point gained.'

The defender doesn't blink when Micko's words of praise for the Waterford boys are relayed back to him.

'Didn't see the man before, during or after the game,' Ogle states bluntly. 'Obviously Micko's a legend but when we are playing them – or his teams – he's just another football man. I have no interest in fawning around him when we play; I just wanted to win that match.'

* * *

Two days later, he pulls into the promenade in Tramore to chat further about the team and its aspirations.

This evening's session has been cancelled because of the death of the former county board secretary, Seamus Grant. The footballers are forming a guard of honour in appreciation of all the work the long-serving official put in over the years. Before he attends the removal, Ogle hits the gym for a punishing two-hour stint, knowing he has to stay on top of his game to keep his place.

'Look, I'd be limited enough as a ball player,' he admits. 'But I have great determination and I put the work in; that helps me compete at this level. There are targets ahead of me now – on Monday night Paul McLoughlin challenged me to score a point from play in every game. That's something for me to work on, and I'll be delighted to try and meet the standard required.'

Ogle doesn't necessarily notice it but in many ways he's one of the main reasons why the team raises the bar higher and higher every season. He missed the entire 2008 season with a cruciate ligament injury and had to fight hard to save his career. His teammates know he personifies everything that's good about them. Since he printed off the minutes from the last players' meeting and reported back to the management, the food after training has already improved and other concerns have been addressed.

He has a diligent manner about him and gets things done without confrontation. Last week, he had a frank chat with the caterers – and while they were not best pleased at their cuisine being criticised by the players, they took some observations on board and the quality of those meals has been enhanced again.

He's also been instrumental in ensuring the team are doing all the right things before games, including enforcing the directive that every player wears the official team gear on the way to games and that they all travel together by bus to away games. In the past fellas were turning up in combats, boiler suits, jeans or tracksuits. These days, they are uniformed.

'Tom Condon rang me last week to see what the players wanted to eat before the Wicklow game and that in itself was great,' he says. 'It shows we're all in this together. So we stopped off in Enniscorthy at 11.30 a.m. and had a choice of pasta and chicken or pasta with tomato sauce and you could have water, brown bread and fruit.

'Up until recent times we would have been getting creamy sandwiches full of mayonnaise and sugar, so it's great to see things shaping up. Christ, it wasn't that long ago that we wouldn't get a thing to eat before a game. I remember stopping off at shops along the way and you'd be buying stuff for yourself, eating all sorts of shite.

'Now we get a good mixture of carbs and protein before games. Sure it has to pay off. If the food isn't right you're at nothing.'

* * *

Since he started out eight years ago, Ogle has noticed a massive change in attitudes.

When they played a promotion-chasing Cavan away from home in 2005 they caused a huge stir by driving one by one into the ground in their own cars. There was even more head-scratching from the locals when they went to a little one-stop shop at the top of Breffni Park and emerged with Mars bars, biscuits and Lucozade bottles. In an era where GAA teams are almost paranoid about their professionalism and appearance, it was like seeing a group of down-and-outs hitting the Waldorf for afternoon tea.

In contrast Cavan were well-groomed and neatly clad in polo shirts and tracksuits. They drove individually to the stadium but then took the team bus to a nearby hotel, where they ate together before travelling back for the match. That's when they saw the Waterford lads looking like Ragball Rovers. While Cavan began their warm-up, their opponents were busily scoffing their stash of goodies. They couldn't but laugh.

In the programme notes, a local journalist, Owen McConnon, wrote that it would be the biggest disaster since the Titanic if Cavan lost that game. They did lose. Ragball Rovers turned them over 0-14 to 1-9.

'Since then, the change in climate has been phenomenal,' Ogle says. 'At the start of this year, management called us in and said that they would provide everything we wanted and they've delivered so far. Now the players realise we have to meet that commitment but more importantly they also realise that we can beat teams, and they know a breakthrough is only around the corner. And it is. So we train together, wear the team uniform and eat properly. No more bullshit.'

The next big treat in store for the team is an extended weekend in London. They play the Exiles on Saturday 14 March but arrangements are being made to turn the weekend into a bonding trip. McLoughlin has already suggested the team and management go camping together in the Comeragh Mountains, while there's another proposal to head off to West Cork for a short spell, but so far a few days across the water looks to be the most popular proposal with the players.

'That's fine, and we'll definitely have a great laugh,' Ogle says. 'On top of that, it's going to be a big deal for us because we never get anything, but there's no way I'm treating it as a piss-up. None of us will be, I can guarantee that. To me, it will be a mini training camp. We'll have a game to win and if we can get a couple of sessions around it, I'll be happy. Then we can all socialise. But until we have the work done, we have no business treating this as a junket. You have to earn those things.'

He teaches Business, Maths and Accounting at De La Salle College in Waterford City and devotes his spare time to looking after six teams there. He's getting married to Deirdre in June 2010 and recently they bought a house together.

Life doesn't crawl idly by for this guy – it speeds in front of him.

Then again, progress doesn't come from standstill men.

Creaming the Cats

15 February, Lemybrien, County Waterford. NFL Round 2

IT'S Valentine's Weekend and Kilkenny are in town for a second-round league clash that's about as romantic as a beef curry.

This is Division 4 football at its bleakest. Today is all about whipping the whipping boys; a chance to rack the scores up against the worst team in Ireland.

In a division that promises to hang on a knife-edge until the very last day, scoring differences will be vital. That's what makes today so important.

From the first minute when Brian Wall shoots a goal Waterford are firmly on top, but it turns out to be one of those games where chance after chance is missed by the home team.

The visitors pack their own half of the pitch and simply hope for the best. Not surprisingly Waterford lead 1-12 to 0-2 at the break but – would you believe it – Eddie Rockett, their centre-back, has scored one of Kilkenny's points.

Just before the break, play broke between the opposition's Eddie Brennan and Thomas O'Gorman, the ball bouncing dangerously on the

21-yard line. Rockett, as usual, was first to sniff out the danger and he arrived quicker than a lawyer at the scene of an accident. Looking at the breaking ball, he put the head down and drew a mighty kick at it. The problem was the kick was aimed in no particular direction.

Taking on a life of its own, the ball soared skyward, Garryowen-like, hung on the breeze for a couple of seconds and then, to Rockett's horror, sailed back towards his own posts, finally landing over the head of a bemused Tom Wall in the Waterford goal. The umpires struggled to control themselves, quivering with suppressed laughter as they raised the white flag.

Astonishingly, this 'own point' raised the Kilkenny dander. 'That's the fucking stuff, lads,' one of their mentors cried. 'Keep the pressure on and they'll fold.'

Rockett stood back and scratched his head as teammates ribbed him mercilessly. He thought he had seen it all as a Waterford footballer. He had now. And not for the first time this season the home bench erupted, once again taking delight in a teammate's misfortune.

'Rockett backfires' is the classic summary offered up by one tabloid comedian.

At the half-time break Kiely storms into the dressing room in mock annoyance and lets his number six have it.

'Jaysus, Rockett, will you at least try to get one at our end this half?' he roars to a chorus of laughter.

But the fun is short-lived. McLoughlin is not happy.

'Eddie, you're a warrior – you should be down there on your knees, smothering that ball into your chest, not drawing an aimless kick at it. If you get hurt, you get hurt,' he fumes.

The mood is suddenly punctured. Tom Wall sees heads dropping and calls for greater patience. 'Jesus, come on, lads, you'd swear we were losing. Come on, keep at it and the scores will come.'

Before they head back out, Kiely offers a gentle reminder of the importance of the game. 'First objective – secure the two points. Then pile on as many scores as you can – scoring difference will be crucial at the end of this competition.'

They proceed to take a hapless Kilkenny apart in the second period and win 2-20 to 0-3 and the 47 supporters in attendance slip out of the ground, no doubt happy with the result but even more delirious that it's all over.

'We have no supporters really,' says Tom Wall. 'You get used to playing in front of no one. I think a lot of people should be ashamed of themselves for not turning out – we're supposed to be a GAA county. A lot of my friends say they will come if the team gives them something to get excited about, but we've had good results in recent years and it doesn't matter a hoot. We're used to it now but it would be nice to have a bit of backing. For most of our home games all you can hear are the opposition fans.

'It's embarrassing. But sure we've enough to be worrying about with the team without worrying about a lack of fans.'

Those who did turn up plonked themselves on the bank right inside the ground, umbrellas at the ready. They are mostly blood relatives of the players and more interested in looking after the children who ramble around playing hide-and-seek, oblivious to the onfield action. Every so often, a ripple of applause announces a home score, but most of the time you just hear the chatter from behind the dugouts. Those who don't have kids to mind are busy texting and getting score updates from the Premiership.

There is scarcely a Kilkenny fan around and not all of their players lasted the full game either; they finished with 13 men after picking up a spate of yellow cards.

At the end of the match, a quick tally reveals that the poor old Cats have now conceded 9-107 in just three games. Little wonder their beleaguered manager, Tom Brennan, is totally disillusioned with the whole thing. It's not easy dealing with one problem at a time when they refuse to get in line.

'It's totally demoralising,' he sighs. 'And we got a few yellow cards there for nothing too. Christ, do the match officials not see that we're only trying to compete? All we want is fair play.'

He pauses, trying to make sense of it all.

'Last year I came in when we had to put a team back in the league and we had a decent enough panel, got a few decent results. But we lost 11 of that squad, and I was talking to John Kiely, who has the same panel for almost five years.

'We come back next year and we'll have a new panel again. We lost two lads to Australia, there are six or seven lads who never came back and two went off to the hurling. The lads who walked away got GPA grant money and never came back. We're obviously short of quality. So it's a labour in vain. Unless Kilkenny lads get back into the business of playing their football championship in June, July and August, which we're not doing, we're at nothing.'

Before seeking refuge on the team bus, he offers his assessment of Waterford: 'Very fit but Antrim and Sligo will go up I'd say. Our lads are training away but we just couldn't stay with Waterford today. Our main problem, though, is that we're not winning kick-outs and our men can't get back with their markers because they're not fit enough. Our full-backs and half-backs have no chance with such little cover in front of them.'

He turns for home but there's one last question. Why bother?

'Well, we take a lot of slagging around the country and in Kilkenny too – I'll get torn asunder when I get home after this. It's bad enough for me but it's the players I feel sorry for. I'm around long enough to take it. My only fear is that lads will walk away for the year ahead. We have another four or five matches left.

'Flying the flag is not enough for me; I actually want to make progress. But I don't know where the answers are or what we're going to do. There's no point in just going out and playing. I'll stick with it, I suppose, for the lads' sake. They won't be thick or tear lumps out of each other after this game but they'll be very down. We're out of our depth. Years ago we had

71

a chance and in several leagues we won three or four games, and now we've a hugely strong division here.'

Brennan's dismay is relayed back to the Waterford set-up but there are no violins produced. To put it bluntly, compassion is in short supply hereabouts.

'It's only four years since we were in that boat ourselves,' Mick O'Loughlin reminds the dressing room. 'Up to two years ago a one-point win over Kilkenny would have been a great result for us. We're not that far out of the woods that we can turn around and be all sympathetic.'

Three points out of four; that's their lot now. And as the players shower and head for the post-match meal at Lawlor's Hotel, they're in good spirits. Amidst the happy chatter, three players innocently reveal how they visited the cinema the night before.

But when they are asked what film was showing, an awkward silence ensues.

Eventually it emerges the movie – *He's Just Not That Into You* – was an out-and-out chick-flick. The image of three gnarled footballers crowding into the cinema on the most romantic night of the year to see a big girl's blouse of a film has the rest of the squad rolling in the aisles.

One by one they depart into the night with wide smiles on their faces. Spirits are high.

There's a three-week break to their next league game. Clare will provide the opposition. It's all good.

Devil's Debut

MICK O'Loughlin's text beeps through and it's straight to the point. 'Training Monday, Wednesday and Friday this week, challenge match against Kildare on Sunday. Next three weeks are most important period of the year. Games v Clare, London and Leitrim ahead. Aim to step up to another level!'

One player who has cruised up through the gears since making his first appearance of the season is the 22-year-old featherweight corner-back Stephen Prendergast, from Kiely's home club, Kilrossanty. Three years ago he debuted for the team against Westmeath and was thrown in at midfield against Rory O'Connell, an All-Star at the time and a player at his peak.

It was like putting Ruby Walsh head to head with John Hayes. He was wiped out of it. Prendergast has lots of talent – he was part of the Irish U-17 International Rules team that toured Australia in 2004 – but he's had an interesting relationship with Waterford football and despite his substantial underage pedigree he hasn't always made the cut. They began this season without him too but the management simply couldn't cope with the huge number of injuries they'd picked up and he was brought in before the start of the league.

It's puzzling that he hasn't developed into the team's star player. Not many Waterford footballers have represented Ireland, and at 23 he should be a mainstay of the team.

Instead he has had to settle for bit parts. Putting a finger on it isn't easy. He blames a disastrous debut, one that left him rattled for a long time after.

'It was the 2006 league clash with Westmeath and I was on the receiving end of a wicked demolition job altogether,' Prendergast concedes. 'Rory O'Connell was one of the best players in Ireland at the time and when he came over to me I knew I was in trouble. To be totally honest, it was the debut from hell. Let's just say I was out of the scene for a while after that.'

Chastened, he chose not to complete his first year with the county. But that's Waterford football for you – easy come, easy go.

Nonetheless, he made another burst to get back in 2007, though that campaign didn't last long either.

'I didn't stick with it, my own fault,' he explains. 'The backroom lads probably saw a fella not putting it in or making the effort and decided to leave me go. You couldn't blame them.'

He is quick to point out that his stagnation hasn't been down to a lack of interest.

'No, I didn't lose my way or go off the rails or anything like that. When I came back from the trip to Australia I probably felt a bit of pressure to stand out with the underage county teams and I wasn't even on the senior panel at that stage. It just took a while to get in but I'm back now and fully intent on making it.'

Taking on board what the rest of the panel asked for in terms of recruiting new blood, Kiely and the backroom decided to take another punt on the young Kilrossanty lad.

Despite not starting in any of the three McGrath Cup matches, he settled well into the camp, impressed in training matches and was picked at left corner-back against Wicklow. His cousin Mark looks after the beat in the opposite corner and thus far the two have been really impressive – sticky, pacy and hard to shake off.

It seems like the kid is ready to take his chance. Relaxed and laid-back, he's always smiling, always buzzing. He never even mentioned playing for Ireland in our chat. That only came to light after a bit of archive-digging. Another lad would still be parading around in his Irish tracksuit.

Ireland won that series in the most dramatic of circumstances. With both teams locked at one test apiece it went down the third and last fixture. Australia were two points down when they went to shoot an over. The referee blew his whistle as the ball left the Aussie player's foot. It sailed over the bar. But the referee disallowed it as he had already blown full-time.

'Ah it was a while ago, but that was serious drama. We went nuts and so did Australia for different reasons,' Prendergast recalls. 'Fantastic, though, it was a great opportunity. To play with fellows like Paul Kerrigan from Cork, Dara Egan from Tipp, Barry Moran, who plays with Mayo, Pádraig Reidy from Kerry – you would learn a lot. They were all on our team. Brendan Quigley and Colm Begley, both of whom were later signed by Aussie Rules teams, were also there. They were a great bunch.'

Ireland played five games, three of them were competitive. These were held in Perth, Brisbane and the Melbourne Cricket Ground. And Prendergast, the young lad from Waterford, played a key role in every one of them. He was mostly at corner-back, though they played an exhibition game against Western Australia and he ended up scoring 1-8 from corner-forward. Their final game was against an Aborigine selection.

Again the Irish dominated. 'That was until they brought out the oval ball for the last quarter,' he laughs. 'It became slightly more competitive after that.'

He'd like to think there are more good times ahead.

'Like I said, you would hope that wasn't the peak of it,' he says, more serious now. 'If I got a settled run maybe I could get back the form I had. But I don't know if I have the speed for corner-back; I play most of my club football at full- or centre-back.'

In the past month he's lost his job and so being a Waterford footballer is a big thing in his life right now. It gives him a focus, something to aim for, keeps him positive.

With only two months to go until he receives his qualification papers, Prendergast, a carpenter by trade, was told to look elsewhere for work. Along with a few others.

For the past four weeks he's been idle, but it's a sign of the times.

'It kind of takes a little bit out of you when you tell people you're unemployed,' he admits. 'I was expecting it, I suppose. Things are gone wicked quiet in our industry, and in the last two months especially it's gone to hell with the private jobs. I was working for a lad and it was very enjoyable but it went. Sure what can you do? I have a few odd jobs lined up and that keeps me ticking over. Put it like this, I haven't spent a week in front of the TV yet looking at Oprah. If that happened it would be time to emigrate.'

He's done his block-work in Cork Institute of Technology and worked with FÁS. And there's a qualification on the way. At least there are options. While he waits for the next move, he can devote all of his energy to football.

'I've already applied to go back to college,' he says. 'No point in hanging around out there if no jobs exist. I may as well go back and sort myself out with another course for two or three years.'

Prendergast is lucky; he doesn't own a house or an expensive car, so the outgoings are small.

'I was going to buy a jeep, a new set of wheels, a while back when things were going well but I didn't and I'm glad now,' he smiles. 'Imagine the bills when you'd be getting no money in at all. I've no mortgage, thank God. So it could be worse. I suppose if I was a Waterford hurler I'd have a better chance of finding work around here but I'll get by for the time being until I see what's in store for me.

'I won't get too stressed. Once you're healthy that's the main thing. I'll tip around doing something until I get sorted.'

This is where sport and Gaelic football come in.

Three nights a week he trains with Waterford and plays a match at the weekend. Being part of a team and enjoying the atmosphere that comes with it takes his mind off other things. He has something to look forward to and targets to meet. Three years ago he 'arsed around', as he puts it. But this year the team tops his agenda.

'Nailing down a place in the full-back line is my aim,' he says. 'And getting promotion is the long-term target. I'm playing alright at the moment but there are bigger tests to come. It's great fun too. The Kilkenny lad I was marking was some craic last weekend. They were making a change on the line and all I could hear was your man under his breath – 'Me, me, me. Jaysus, please take me off'. He was getting fierce agitated when it looked like they were taking off the other corner-forward. Then they flashed up his number and he couldn't contain himself any longer. He let a big roar – 'Yes!' – when they called him ashore. I don't think we were ever that bad.'

Before he heads off, he admits he has plenty to work on.

'I have to work hard on my speed, that's my biggest problem, but I'll stick with it now. We have Kildare on Sunday in a challenge match so that will be a huge one. You never know I could even twinge my hamstring for that – it might be safer than marking some shit-hot corner-forward,' he jokes.

He might have pulled a fast one a few years ago, but this is a different Stephen Prendergast that Waterford have on their books now.

No more hiding.

Chapter 6

The Coach from Clane (Paul McLoughlin's Story)

The Kildare Years

I managed to stay off the fags for 18 years but it all went out the window when I took this bloody job.

In the past few weeks I'm back on the cursed things again. That's what the McGrath Cup will do to you. Back in the habit.

I tend to get a bit edgy before games so that might explain it. I was especially tense before the Wicklow match. Jackson saw me and came over laughing, telling me to relax, that I was a typical Kildareman, nervous as a kitten on the big day. But the bottom line is that I've been sucked right into this. I want to do well with the lads and for the lads. There is pressure. So the odd fag helps.

I'm not a placid man anyway. In fact when it comes to football I'd be pretty thick. Anyone from my hometown of Clane would verify that and they mightn't be too complimentary about me either. But there's no point in being something you're not. I've had a fiery streak since I started playing football with Kildare. I was with them for 10 years and to this day people harp on about us being the hard-luck story of the 1990s.

I don't go along with that. The truth is we just weren't good enough.

Don't get me wrong – we weren't a million miles away, but back then we simply couldn't get past Meath or Dublin. Meath were winning All-Irelands and any team that wanted to lift Sam Maguire also had to beat Dublin along the way. In that era, you lost one championship game and it was curtains.

Still, we got a lift when Mick O'Dwyer took over for the first time. People hone in on this myth and aura surrounding him but boiling it down to brass tacks, he simply got me fitter than I ever was before. Simple as that. And I learned not to have my tea before I went training. If I did eat, Micko's survival-camp training regime ensured I'd see my supper again very soon.

Under his system all I needed was a five-second break in play and I was ready to show for the ball again. The interesting thing is that I never once got tired playing a match for him. Afterwards, though, I'd be in an absolute heap and I would have to hop into bed to sleep a bit. But during games it was non-stop.

He educated Kildare players and told us what it took to win. We had some good managers before he came – people like John Courtney and Dermot Earley – but some players didn't listen to them, didn't make what was needed in terms of sacrifice. We just didn't put it in.

I had a good few lowlights in the Kildare shirt but that's the way it goes. We nearly won a national league title in 1991, Micko's first year, but ultimately lost our way in the final. Looking back, I think if the current qualifier system had been in place back then we could have been a force in the championship, but there's no point reminiscing now.

On the club scene, I played for Clane until 1998, when we were beaten in the Leinster series. Then I took over as manager. I'd have been very feisty as a player and would have mouthed a lot during games so I wouldn't have been everyone's cup of tea. But I was asked to do the job and I agreed.

It was an enjoyable few years and later on I trained St Kevin's in Kildare before being transferred down to Wexford with the Army. While there, I took charge of Grangemockler in Tipperary and had a great time. You get the picture – no matter where I went there was always football.

All in all I spent 23 years with the Army and then it was time for a change. Five years ago we made our move, my wife and I. We moved to Waterford and set up a business: the Handmade Furniture Company.

Of course football soon followed.

Mango and The Legend

Late in 2008 I was asked to join the Waterford set-up and since then it's dominated my life. I absolutely love it. Whether I feel the same in a month or six weeks' time remains to be seen but so far I have a really good feeling about this.

When they asked me to come on board, it only took about five minutes to make up my mind.

We were sitting in the Granville Hotel on the city quay, drinking coffee and chatting about a whole range of things. At some stage the conversation turned to football. Mick O'Loughlin and John Kiely asked if I was interested in working with them. I double-checked one or two things just to see what the structures were like, but once we were all on the same hymn sheet, I agreed. Didn't even take time to think about it.

People wondered if I'd lost the plot. Waterford football? Division 4 no-hopers. I'd heard it all.

But so what? I had my homework done and knew they had some decent players. Once it was clear that we were all on the same level, I was in.

I have my schedule now. By day it's business and by night it's football.

We have a shop on the city quay. We make our own furniture in Indonesia, mostly with mango wood, transport it over to Ireland and sell it over three levels of our store. It's all our own design and work. Once a month, we get this great big container delivered and have to come in at 5 a.m. to stock up. We had a warehouse but we let it go because of the recession, just to reduce costs. When the economy dipped every businessman and businesswoman in the land had to cut back on almost everything. Better to be safe and all that.

It's all about survival now but hopefully we will get through it. We have a good name and a good reputation but the next few years will test every small business in Ireland.

Folks were asking if I hadn't enough on my plate without taking on this coaching role but I actually relished the chance to get stuck into it. Because I'm self-employed I'm obviously under pressure with the recession. And it's just bloody marvellous that, come 6 p.m., I can lock up, go away to training and forget all about it. I can go away to train the Waterford team, be part of an adventure. And it is an adventure.

The Backroom Power

Any dealings with Jackson would put you in good form. His reputation – or legend, should I say – went before him. I knew bits about him from the local press but after being in his company for a few minutes I saw a different side. He could be ruthless too.

Sure, he might be Mr Personality and really popular with everyone but straightaway I could see that he wanted to get out of Division 4.

And while I was going down the ladder a few levels footballwise, you could see the great improvements he has made over the years. When they knocked on my door, I don't think they were looking for any fresh expertise, just another angle.

It's more or less attention to detail that wins games – you have 50 things to get right before you win a match. If you get 36 of them right you have a chance of winning, if you get 40 things right you have a really good chance and very occasionally you will get everything right. Maybe they just wanted to tick a few more boxes and reckoned a new voice could help them.

John was very disarming but it struck me pretty quickly that he was also a real thinking GAA fellow. He's fierce thoughtful. Mick is equally important and he really wanted me on board so there was never any

81

question of a conflict or crossover between the two of us. His role is vital. The only injuries we've had are guys who've done nothing for four or five months and come back and get niggles. That's down to him. And our fitness levels have always matched those teams we've played. That's down to him too.

The infrastructure? Well, floodlights are vital for intense ball-work and peripheral-vision preparation – the lights simply have to be good enough. Seemingly, that aspect wasn't great up to 2009 but we have it rectified now. Another box ticked.

From the start, my brief was simple. The lads had done a lot of development work but I have my own ideas, regimes and tactics.

I lean very heavily on Ulster coaching practices, but the players tell me things as they go along too. In training, Eddie Rockett and the likes have come up and told me face to face what they wanted. If I'm not doing the business they let me know. It's player-driven to a great extent and I have no problem with that because it means there's passion.

Does it lessen the backroom team's power? Not at all – it shows we respect them; they are our players. That compromise must now exist with teams all over the country.

Truth be told, though, I've actually learned a lot from them. The players run the show in most counties, from what I can see, and if you want to make progress you have to listen to them.

Overall, from the first night I turned up at training, everything was more or less as I expected it to be. The facilities were okay and once the lads were getting looked after with meals and gear, and once we had floodlights, I was happy.

Early days, it looked like we had Gary Hurney and I was making great plans for him. In the end, though, I knew he and the other lads would all leave us to go with Davy Fitzgerald. You can't blame them really. There were 7,000 or 8,000 at the hurlers' league match against Kilkenny, whereas there would only actually be 7 or 8 in total at our games. The hurlers have the razzmatazz. They were close in 2008, apart from a bad day in the All-Ireland final, and the interest down here is massive. If you're in Division 4 here and they're in an All-Ireland final you know what path the dual players will choose.

A real pity about Gary, though. I saw serious potential in him. If he was playing regularly and getting games every week, he had the ability to be as good as Matty Forde. You could see what he's capable of, but if you're not playing consistently at the right level you can't judge how good he actually is. When he left, I witnessed at first-hand the fight the boys have on their hands to keep everyone together. And it's made me admire them even more.

But he's gone, there's nothing we can do and even if there was an inkling that he was coming back, it would be up to the players to decide if he would be let return.

There are no guarantees anymore – that's how far they've all come.

Working as a Team

Apart from all that, the biggest problem that needed to be addressed was getting the lads to play like a team. Teamwork, support play and supporting the man on the ball – they were all desperately poor, to be honest, and needed sorting out. Lads were going off on hospital runs with no one with them. Now, even if lads are tired, they make a support run to drag an opponent away and at the very least they make space. I'd like to think we've improved on that aspect. Our shooting is still woeful at times, though, and we simply don't seem to be able to fist a handy ball over the bar. That needs work quickly.

Being so close, I can't really see a week-to-week improvement but maybe we don't need to lift it all that much. I reckon we could feasibly win the next four games and if we did, it would really set the cat among the pigeons.

What surprises me, day-in day-out, is the lads' commitment. They're doing more training than a lot of counties higher up the register – four days a week – and strength-and-conditioning too. You could say it's five days.

I try to keep things fresh by having a lot of mini games, four against five, five against five and four against four. You can play a couple of ongoing games at the same time and get a lot done. Condition games, they are called. They make the players perform more efficiently by laying down certain rules.

I do a fair bit of research on what works and what doesn't but the best drills are the ones off the Ulster GAA website. It's a brilliant site and they have special coaching DVDs to watch as well. On top of that, I know Mick McGeehan from Coaching Ireland and the Donegal football team and he has given me a lot of exercises to help teamwork. We make those drills and games that we've been told about as intensive as possible.

In return, our boys have done everything we've asked.

I would love to have a natural corner-forward, a guy who just stays inside and pops two or three points over the bar every day. But they don't grow on trees. There's a young lad called Brian O'Halloran from Clashmore who is the best we have but the lads won't bring him in because he's still a minor. I'd have him in with us this second. You can improve a lot of things but you really can't make a player a finisher. We can sharpen them up alright and we're doing that. We've started to bring in yoga, we have a strength-and-conditioning coach, a stamina coach, but we can't do everything.

So Brian Wall and Sean Fleming are two forwards we've focused on for shooting practice and they're shaping up well lately. Finishing under pressure is only something that clicks when you have a bit of experience and practice, so maybe as the weeks go on, we might unearth a few more sharpshooters.

As the whole thing has taken off I've been plunged deeper into it. We were worried at the start about the poor numbers at training and I wondered if this was the future. These guys are Division 4 men all their lives. They've been hammered inside and outside of Waterford, so we couldn't dictate to them. We were easy on them, egged them along, and now we have a full complement.

People were saying John and the lads were under pressure to keep their jobs last year (in 2008) but I wouldn't do this if the lads weren't here. If they are not here in 2010 I won't be either.

John makes all the tough decisions and makes it all tick. All good managers back their players, like Alex Ferguson or Seán Boylan. They might say certain things in private but publicly they are loyal.

John is ready to make the tough decisions. His thought process before games is impressive. He doesn't go on the Internet to research and he may be old-fashioned, but every week he gets eight or nine local papers from all over the country delivered to the shop in Lemybrien and he'd quote you chapter and verse on the form of any player in Ireland.

I've definitely learned way more from them on how to deal with players – what methods work and what don't. Our players can see through bullshit. And deep down they all have doubts about their ability, so I've learned how to make points in a constructive fashion rather than losing my head. You can't be telling them where they are going wrong all the time. A lot of that happens in GAA and in life too. It's an Irish thing.

The way it works down here? Have it out. Tell them straight. Five seconds later we all move on. No time for falling out with anyone.

We're all in this together. I feel as if I've been with them for years now.

Chapter 7
Another Bogey Team Dealt With

The Kid from CIT
—•—

28 February, Cork IT campus, County Cork

SEÁN O'HARE slants back in his seat and ruffles his hair. Looks around the room. Yawns. He hasn't had much sleep.

Last night was nuts. Cork Institute of Technology (CIT) won the Sigerson Cup and he was in the middle of it. Literally. They beat DCU and NUI Galway, and O'Hare, a Division 4 player, now has a Sigerson medal. John Kiely has gone away to enquire if there's another native out there who has won one but he's doubtful.

'If one exists he's kept fairly quiet about it,' the manager surmises.

When O'Hare's Sundays are free forever, he'll look back with fondness on this feat. He missed Waterford's pre-season tournament games because he was cup-tied and bound to play all the McGrath Cup clashes with the college but Kiely didn't mind. Early reports from Cork indicated their man was settling in well and his football was beginning to glow.

The Kid has all the skills that will make him a top footballer. Blessed with a tremendous leap, the youngster is built like a brick wall; he could run all day and can pinch a point or two on the run. In fact he's one of the few players on Kiely's team who is comfortable shooting from distance while in full flight.

In many ways it's fitting that a Waterford man has shared in CIT's success. Both teams have travelled on back roads meandering through the heart of the GAA but gradually, the college has worked its way out of the shadows and onto centre stage.

Until recently they weren't even allowed compete in the red letter college competitions but now they're King of the Hill, top of the heap.

Compared to other more illustrious rivals they have small numbers, a population of only 5,500 or so, but nearly 10 per cent are members of their GAA club. It's a family unit; they don't go blatantly poaching players and they also encourage students to get involved in administration as well as coaching. The idea is that their graduates will continue to be involved in the GAA when they toss their hats in the air.

With nearly the entire 2009 team eligible for defence of the Sigerson in 2010, they will continue to be a force and for his part, O'Hare, a second-year Structural Engineering student, is hoping he will have at least another three years playing in the red and white shirt.

At the start he wasn't sure if he was good enough but there was a trial game against Jordanstown and they told him if he had designs on making any shapes he had better be there. The same weekend, he was playing an U21 county hurling final with his club Abbeyside but it cut no mustard. If he wanted to make the CIT team, he was to be in Jordanstown.

Make it he did. He won his hurling match, keyed the northern destination point into the Sat Nav and travelled up the country. It was worth it; he got a start at midfield and still buzzing from the U21 final win, played a blinder. They weren't able to leave him off after that.

'When I walked into the dressing room there was nothing only Cork and Kerry fellows and if I'm being honest they looked down on me and I looked up to them. Because I was from Waterford. But after a while it was obvious

I could hold my own. I got a bit of respect and started getting to know the lads,' he says.

'Our main man is the Cork forward, Daniel Goulding, but there are a heap of other guys from the main footballing counties with intercounty experience. I learned an awful lot from the likes of them. There are lots of differences between Sigerson and Division 4 football. The main one is the pace of the college game where you have young lads flying all over the pitch at a really high tempo. It's fast and furious, wide open and the ball is sprayed all over the park. My job is to sit in the middle of the field and protect those behind me. We have a very strict game-plan and even though I would enjoy bursting forward whenever I could, I wouldn't be allowed do it.'

There are no such restrictions with the county senior side. Even though he's a novice in his first year, O'Hare has something of a free rein. That's life when you have a big name in a small world.

'For a start, we are much more guarded and cautious in our style of play,' he reckons. 'The main thing is to crowd our defence and try to cut down on conceding scores. I'm not restricted or anything like that, I can move up and down the field, but we go very deep and you can't really let the ball go first time because it won't stick up there.

'That can be frustrating. The intensity in Division 4 is not as intense as it is playing against the likes of DCU and that, but at the same time it can be harder to get a score because there are so many bodies in front of you.'

O'Hare hopes that the success is only the first of three goals he has set himself for 2009. The first box has been ticked, the second is to help Waterford get out of Division 4 and the third target is to complete his second-year exams with merit. He's ambitious but you grow great with your dreams.

'I have 34 hours a week with lots of projects and it's very intense,' he says. 'I missed out on a fair bit of study with the football but I'm back into it now and travelling to Waterford for training at least one night a week. I

Jackson's Grand Entrance: Waterford manager John Kiely makes his way onto the Kill GAA pitch for the second round of the McGrath Cup against UL.

Sideline marshal: Kiely walks the line in his side's NFL encounter with Leitrim.

The backroom boys: (L-R) Kiely, Tom Condon, Paul McLoughlin, Mick O'Loughlin and Ger Power make their way off the field after a convincing late show gave them full points against Carlow.

Stephen 'Budgie' Cunningham. 15 championship seasons with Waterford and just one win.

Liam Lawlor. Scottish-based university student and former Waterford senior hurler who flew over and back from Edinburgh for games during the season.

Munster interprovincial player. Thomas O'Gorman. We think. On a good day only his family members can tell him apart from twin Maurice.

Cillian O'Keeffe. Probably the lightest player in intercounty football but one of the bravest too.

Wayne's World: The multi-talented Wayne Hennessy, footballer, hurler and soccer player.

'Small' Tom Wall. The team's goalkeeper who went nine games and almost two seasons without conceding a league goal.

Ger Power, Selector. A former Waterford footballer and one of Jackson's most trusted lieutenants.

Seeing double. The brilliant twins Maurice and Thomas O'Gorman.

Grub's up. Seán O'Hare, Conor McGrath and Liam Lawlor await this culinary delight, courtesy of a local caterer.

Tucking in: Ger Power, Tony Grey and Stephen Cunningham get stuck into their post-training meal in the dressing room before they make their way home from Fraher Field.

Pep talk. Jackson addresses the team before they tackle Leitrim.

Tactics talk. Wearing a Barcelona cap, Kiely discusses a move with Ger Power during the Leitrim match.

Pride after a fall. Jackson congratulates the team after a win against Leitrim puts them back in the promotion frame again.

Us against the world. The team huddle tightly before their crucial NFL 'do or die' encounter with Sligo.

Hiding to nothing. The team trot out onto Fraher Field for their Munster championship opener against Cork in May, having scarcely trained together five times in the previous month.

Hot streak. Sharpshooter Liam Ó Líonáin celebrates his fourth goal of the NFL campaign with a sensational strike that clinched a win over Mickey Morrisson's Leitrim.

Warming Up. Tony Grey and Mark Prendergast go through their paces before the start of the team's championship match with Cork.

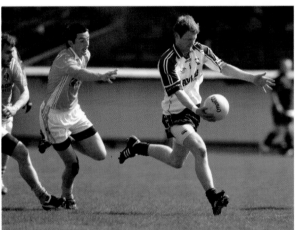

Don't stop me now: Liam Ó Líonáin in full flight against Antrim in the team's final NFL game.

If we don't have each other, who do we have? The team rally before playing Carlow in the NFL.

Jackson and Paul McLoughlin make their final points to the team before their win over Leitrim.

Easy does it. Stephen Cunningham gets a stretch of the hamstring with the help of team physio Cian O'Connor.

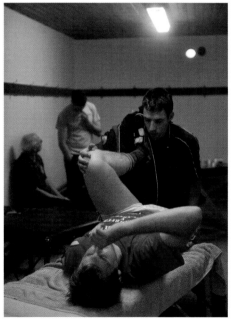

Repeat exercise. Cian O'Connor works the oracle on Seán O'Hare who played for seven teams, including club, college and county in both hurling and football, during the 2009 season.

Diehards. Only the brave and faithful turn out to watch the team. Most of those present were there to support Leitrim, the visiting side.

Sign of the times. Waterford are no longer the whipping boys. Poor Kilkenny now possess that most unfortunate tag.

All done bar the talking. With the preparations for another championship complete, all that Jackson, Ger Power, Paul McLoughlin, Ollie Drummy (Fraher Field groundsman) and Tom Condon can do is hope the team perform well against Cork.

The Underdog. Jackson chats to Dubliner Glen Kelly, Waterford's reserve goalkeeper who made his name on the TG4 *Underdogs* show.

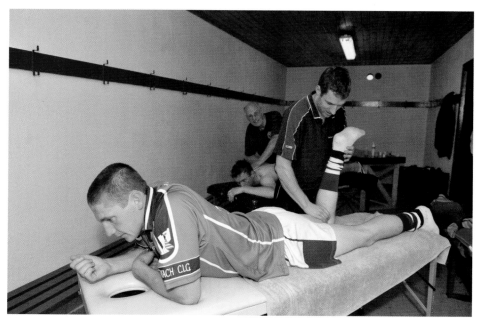

'Andy to have around. Veteran Andy Hubbard came out of retirement during the season to lend Kiely a hand when numbers were depleted. He is pictured here receiving a rub on his calves from physio Cian O'Connor.

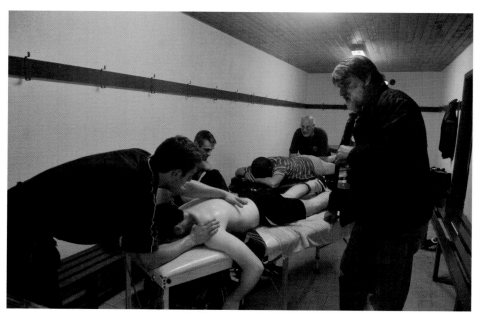

'I don't give a shite if you're injured, get back out there.' Or words to that effect. Jackson checks out the fitness of his goalkeeper Tom Wall.

Golden boot. Liam Ó Líonáin ended the year as one of the top scorers from play in the country with 6-15 to his name in the NFL.

Comeback kid. Defender Shane Briggs (Briggsy) returned from a cruciate ligament injury in time for the 2009 season.

Mick Ahearne. The brilliant midfield general with almost a decade of service in the Waterford shirt saw his 2009 season destroyed by a mystery virus.

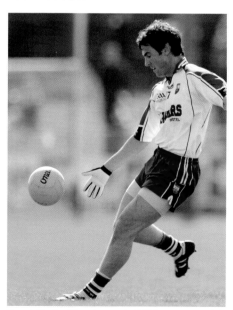

Paul Ogle. The team's GPA rep saw his championship aspirations go up in flames when he ruptured a cruciate ligament for the second time in nine months – just as he was rediscovering his best form.

Gary Hurney. The 'dual' in the crown, Hurney was under pressure to line out with the county hurlers and footballers in 2009. He tried to combine both until a broken collarbone ruled him out of the football qualifier with Meath and the Munster hurling final and subsequent All-Ireland quarter-final.

Long-serving defender John 'Fifi' Phelan made his return to the team having missed the early stages of the season due to his marriage and subsequent honeymoon.

Word in your ear. Jackson tries to sweet-talk Clare referee Rory Hickey in the team's final league clash with Antrim.

Grey's battery. After an injury-plagued start to the season, the relentless work rate of wing back Tony Grey earmarked him as one of the team's brightest prospects.

Captain call. Maurice O'Gorman and Philip Roche shake hands before their one-sided league encounter in Lemybrien. The dark skies tell all you need to know about this game.

Jason Ryan. Waterford football's most famous export took over the Wexford football team in 2008 and incredibly led them to an All-Ireland semi-final. His only regret was that his new managerial job meant having to pack up playing with his native county.

A Year on the Road with Waterford

Leitrim
21 March

Sligo
12 April

Meath
4 July

Wicklow
7 January

Clare
4 March

Tipperary
2 June

Carlow
28 March

Kilkenny
4 January

London
14 March

Waterford
4 January

Cork
24 May

don't see any reason why we cannot get promotion. There isn't a whole lot between the teams. Looking down the line I think we should have three more wins in the bag before we meet Sligo away, which will be a very difficult proposition. But I think we can take Antrim at home. It's there for us, I wouldn't be too negative about our chances at all.

'I do have some concerns, though. We tend to fall very far back if we make a mistake or concede a couple of scores. That has to be rectified. Nothing can be perfect all the time in a game and lads lose heart very easily. But if we can guard against that we might be OK.'

Still only 22, he's learning all the time from his teammate and minder, Mick Ahearne, in the heart of the Waterford engine room.

'The one thing I've seen at first-hand is that if I make a mistake "Mickah" is there to clean up straight away and sort it out. He's awesome to play with, up and down the field, and he takes some hits. Mind you, he's well able to dish them out too. I think we've developed a tight understanding in the past two or three games.'

Ahearne has devoted a large chunk of his life to plucking Waterford from the depths of Division 4. Now O'Hare could help slay the popular caricature that portrays them as lazy no-hopers. It might be some time before Aherne hands over the responsibility but when that time comes The Kid will be ready to take the baton.

The Lilywhite Limber-up

2 p.m., 8 March, Cusack Park, Ennis, County Clare, NFL Round 3

A HALF-HOUR to throw in and the mood is flat in this drab and grey dressing room. Too flat.

The players have been on their feet since early that morning, some of them assembling as early as 10 a.m. to fetch the bus from Dungarvan. They haven't stopped along the way to grab a pre-match meal and that's a mistake; you can tell they're a little unsettled. Nervous energy is always welcome before a game but the prevailing mood in here is anxiety.

Two points are badly needed today. Without them you can more or less bid farewell to promotion, even at this early stage of the season. The stakes are that high. This afternoon, Sligo are away to London and Antrim will be fancied to beat Leitrim. Wicklow are away to Kilkenny and they'll pull themselves back into the race. So Waterford have got to keep the momentum.

It's been three weeks since their last outing but in that time they took on Kildare in a challenge match and they've prepared well. The challenge was played in Tinryland, just off the M9, and at one stage it looked like it might be better for all concerned if it never went ahead. Even in the warm-up you could tell the difference between the teams – Waterford were going through their pre-match drills in earnest enough fashion but the pace of Kildare's limber-up was simply ferocious. They were thumping seven shades of shite out of each other before a ball was even thrown in.

And though their manager Kieran McGeeney wasn't even there, you could see there was a raw honesty in their build-up.

No shock then that they surged seven points ahead before Waterford even copped there was a game on. The worst thing was that save for Mick Wright, Emmet Bolton and Killian Brennan, there weren't even that many recognisable faces on the Lilywhite team. As the game progressed word reached the Waterford sideline that most of the opposition comprised senior panellists or else intermediate players jousting for positions on McGeeney's squad. It was chastening to say the least.

Eventually though, Kiely's men got to grips with the affair and only lost 2-20 to 2-12 in the end – not the worst of beatings. The positives? Ger Power got the bones of a full game in on his road to recovery and Liam Ó Líonáin's scorching pace left the Kildare defence in a twist, time and time again. Mick Ahearne put in his best display of the season as he knocked Kildare men out of the way like they were pests in his face.

But once again deficiencies in the Waterford team were highlighted. It turned out to be a disjointed, patternless dog of a game. When faced with a high tempo, Waterford could not cope and were stretched from one side of the field to the other. Their short-passing rhythm missed a beat in the final quarter of attack and they missed far too many scoring chances.

Still, the management left for home reckoning it was better to learn from their mistakes rather than hiding the cracks by playing inferior opposition. There is a train of thought, though, that they've over-trained and with that in mind they opt to take it easy over the next seven days.

The following Monday night Colin Kelly spins down from Louth to work on their shooting and they wound up preparations for Clare with another short and sharp session two evenings later. After running like Kenyans for the previous month, it's time to wind down. They want to be bursting at the seams for the Ennis encounter.

And so here we are: Clare in their own backyard, where many a big scalp has been claimed over the years. Kiely has picked a really strong side but this is sport, this is Gaelic football and as a manager you live and die by the strength of the team dynamic. It's seldom that stays fully intact.

The night before the game the manager receives a phone call. The O'Gorman brothers are out. Their father, John, is suffering from sickness and is in his final hours. Obviously, the three lads are in no frame of mind to play. Just last year they lost their mother. Life has dealt them an incredibly tough hand. This latest horrendous setback has left the entire camp numb.

Kiely fizzes down the hushed corridors, takes to the floor and faces his men. A deep sadness prevails across the dressing room.

'As you know, there are some enforced changes,' he says. 'You all know about the O'Gormans' terrible news. Their father doesn't have long and they're in our thoughts.

'It puts sport into perspective,' he continues, 'but at the same time it's the reason why we're all here. A good few of us have experienced tragedy and sadness over the past year or two. There are a few men in this dressing room who have been touched by great sadness in the past 12 months and I've experienced that myself with the loss of my own father. For Maurice, Thomas and Michael it's even harder because they only lost their mam last year.

'So our hearts and thoughts go out to them, they are Waterford footballers, part of us, and they've been struck harder than any of us could ever imagine.

'This is why we play sport lads. To get away from it all. Every one of us who has experienced sadness in our lives, we've always turned to sport. I know I got great solace and comfort from my GAA friends when my father passed away. I'm still struggling to deal with it but the comfort comes in being able to come in here and do something you love. So we'll be there for the lads when they come back. And keep them in your thoughts. We have to work around the fact that they're not here.

'Justin Seaward comes in at full-back and John Phelan comes in at right half-back. And with Maurice not here, our captain for the day is Mick Ahearne.'

Kiely takes another step back and fixes a steely glare at Ahearne, one of his trusted lieutenants, his eyes glittering at the memory of his midfielder putting his body on the line for the cause on numerous occasions over the past five years.

'Mick, you're the first Kill man to captain the Waterford footballers and can I just say there's not a man who deserves it as much as you.' The room fills with emotion and the players burst into a spontaneous round of applause. Ahearne, a no-fuss character, nods his head, his brow painted with lines of concentration.

Kiely finishes off his speech with an in-depth player by player review of the opposition. 'Inexperienced, full of youngsters, nothing we haven't faced before,' he summarises. 'Play as a team, work hard and play smart. Go out and bring the two points home.'

Of course, it wouldn't be a Kiely sermon without some bit of mischief.

He addresses Eddie Rockett.

'Their centre-back Kevin Dilleen is not long back from the hurlers,' he points out. 'He's only with them a short while and a few of their players are back after walking out in a bit of a sulk a few weeks ago. So Rocky, I'll leave it to you to have a few words in the ears of those lads. You can chat to them yourself; you always know what to say.'

Now there's laughter and it breaks the ice, lifts the spirits. They egg each other on and at 2.15 p.m. they break onto the field for the pre-match warm up. The first breaths of spring haven't been friendly thus far and dark clouds hover over Ennis with flakes of snow softly falling from the skies.

Bring Home the Two Points

In the stands four Waterford supporters, die-hards, shout encouragement from the moment the team hits the field. In total there are 250 spectators gathered and the majority reckon there's an easy home win on the cards. They see no reason to change their minds when Frank Doherty's side march 0-4 to 0-0 ahead after 15 minutes.

Clare are pumped up; they've endured a rotten start to the season and before the game they tuned into RTÉ Radio One to hear that the Waterford players fancied themselves big time and backed themselves heavily to win at two-and-a-half to one. Presenter Con Murphy asks studio guest John Maughan if such a practice is allowed and Maughan confirms it's acceptable – as long as a team backs itself to win.

The strange thing is that none of the players have even thought about a bet and equally the subs in the stand are at a loss to explain where the rumours stemmed from. Anyone following Gaelic football over the past few years would have spotted the excellent value being offered by the bookies and experienced gamblers would certainly have backed a Waterford win heavily. From there, idle gossip is born.

Right now, though, the odds look accurate. Waterford are a team with no middle setting. They either run full throttle or they don't run at all. For the first 15 minutes they don't really run at all. Their passing is atrocious and their shooting even worse. Somehow, Liam Ó Líonáin drives a ball wide from about seven yards out. More than any, Liam Ó mirrors his team's performance. When he's in the mood, he can run riot. When he's not, he gets disheartened and loses concentration, tries too hard.

The rest are faring no better. Seán Fleming can't get a look in. Most of the other forwards are stuck in their own defence. Eventually, Paul Ogle, who has been moved from wing-back to centre-forward for this match, clips over a point.

It seems to flick a switch.

Gradually, they find their rhythm, passing regularly out of defence, working their way up to the attack, rolling away to find a loose man and working the ball into a shooting position.

By the interval they're only 0-8 to 0-7 behind, with a gale-force wind at their backs for the second half but they can thank Tom Wall for that. The diminutive keeper makes two excellent stops to keep his team in it. The first is a point-blank save from his near post, the second a thing of unrefined beauty. He spread himself like an eagle in front of Clare full-forward Michael O'Shea and clawed a goal-bound certainty out of harm's way.

It might sound crazy but already it's clear Waterford are the better side. Apart from the robotic free-taking skills of David Tubridy, Clare, for all their huff and puff, are extremely limited.

Inside Paul McLoughlin speaks to his players and stirs the fire again.

'A gale-force wind against us and we're only a point behind,' he says, 'and the beauty is that we haven't even started playing yet. We've made mistakes, not played to our best but these lads are wilting. You are by far the better fucking team. They thought ye were dead and buried at the start but look at the balls you showed to fight back.'

He walks out to join the rest of the backroom team but pauses. Heads are dropped. It's like they've already lost. He needs to get them motoring again.

'Hey lads,' he shouts back at them with a clinched fist. 'We're still good, aren't we?'

It works. They respond collectively. He has roused them.

Standing on their feet they begin to cajole each other again, reassuring the man beside them that they are, in fact, the better team. All those years in the doldrums have implanted deep insecurities in the minds of the more experienced players. It's as if one or two mistakes in a game completely knocks the stuffing out of them.

'Don't mind the fucking mistakes,' Liam Lawlor advises. 'Play the game we've practiced. We'll always make mistakes in games but continue making the runs and space will appear.'

Rockett and Ogle add their tuppence worth but one of the more interesting contributors to the half-time discussion is Shane Briggs, a schoolteacher and the team's regular centre-back, who has just recovered from a cruciate injury. Briggs is gasping to get back onto the field but the management won't allow his thirst to be quenched just yet.

With this blunt analysis, he nails the problem at the root of Waterford's stop-start first half.

'Every time Clare get on the ball they have men fucking crying out for it,' he observes. 'The simple truth – if ye're looking for it – is that they are hungrier than ye are. Take that whatever way ye want but if ye don't match them in the second half for hunger, it's curtains.'

There's no bitching; the rest of the players agree.

Last year, Clare took them in the championship but this time, with the breeze in their backs, Waterford will not be stopped.

'Lads, play to the game-plan; the wind never won anything for anyone,' Kiely quips as they head out the door.

And then, just as they get ready to break back onto the field, a lovely moment materialises.

The players and subs meet at the door and face each other in the eye. They clap the man next to them, they huddle up and wheedle each other. Then they dart back onto the field. And for the next 35 minutes, save one or two squeaky bum moments, they boss the game. It's not vintage stuff but they do enough to win 0-15 to 0-12.

As they warm down, stretching their hamstrings and groins, the delight is etched all over their faces.

'Another bogey team dealt with,' Tom Wall, the hero of the hour, notes as he hugs his teamates.

Eye on London

Although still aligned to the right track, it's again clear that certain areas of the team need urgent servicing if they are to flee the bottom tier. A lot of players have underperformed and poor passing has affected the game-plan. It's been a hugely frustrating day for O'Hare just a week after his college exploits. He struggled to get going and received a yellow card during the second half. Under the experimental rules his day ended before he even got going. For a player the rest of the team were looking up to, you can see from his expression that he feels he has let them down. He spent the last 20 minutes of the game with his head in his hands, just hoping that they could carve out that win.

As they hit the showers, they can hear the opposing players next door get a bollicking and a half from their manager Frank Doherty. Someone roars that Clare football is at an all-time low. The Waterford lads hear this but they're not in the least bit insulted – it's just another reminder of how far they've come.

There's still a stigma attached to losing to Waterford. No matter that they've beaten the likes of Cavan, Antrim, Wexford and Leitrim over the past couple of seasons. No matter that they've run Kerry to eight points in the Munster championship.

Nah, they're still regarded as the 30th best team in Ireland, slightly ahead of London and Kilkenny. The bookies don't give them any credit and rivals still reckon that dropping points to them is the lowest ebb in their own history.

However, as they board the bus and head for the Clare Inn for a post-match meal, their hair still wet from the showers, the players don't mind in the least. Five points out of six. How bad.

The following morning John O'Gorman, the father of the lads, passes away and his death leaves the family mourning the loss of a second parent since August the previous year. It truly does put sport in perspective. The brothers' teammates rally around and attend the removal on Tuesday evening and funeral the following morning. They provide as much comfort as they can.

And then they give the O'Gormans their privacy and go back to their own lives to prepare for the next match, well aware that sport also provides us with a respite from our worries.

While their three teammates, fine quiet lads, try to pick up the pieces, the rest of the squad looks ahead to the weekend where another two points are up for grabs.

This time London's calling.

With the economy floundering here, it's no surprise that the GAA in London has received a new injection of life. It's not door-to-door salesmen Tommy Harrell has to contend with; it's the surge of ex-pats arriving to his house with transfer forms. Harrell has devoted his life to administering the affairs of hurling and football across the water and has scuffled along for decades without much success, keeping the exiled family together but with only bad times looming in Ireland, he could now experience a second coming.

Last year, London sent over a team of second-generation Irish kids to play Waterford in the league and they were stuffed. They are a different entity this time, with three former Galway footballers already in their ranks.

Jackson is taking them very seriously and wonders if it's time to give his old friend Jason Ryan a call.

These days, 32-year-old Ryan is better known as the wonder kid of intercounty management having guided Wexford from the edge of darkness to the radiance of an All-Ireland semi-final. He's hot property – young, slick and full of ideas.

But to Kiely he'll always be Jason. The lad who rung him when he came home from London, looking to play a bit of ball with Waterford. One of the warriors he came to depend upon.

Chapter 8
Born to Run
(Jason Ryan's Story)

Paco & the Perks

I HAVE a confession to make: I was never actually invited onto the Waterford panel – I rang to ask could I join. That's not normally how players make their intercounty debut but that's how it was with me.

As a kid, I played county minor football and Paco Curran was our manager. I headed off to London for 10 years and when I came back he was a senior selector. So I rang him and asked if I could come in.

We always got on great. Paco was into goal-setting and would go around the dressing room before games issuing targets to each player. Before him, the main target for a Waterford player was to show up for a game. I loved his style.

He knew I'd be fiercely committed and he agreed to let me train with them. And just to be sure, I cleared it with Jackson. It was his first year as manager and I didn't want to be upsetting him. But Paco had paved the way and everything was fine.

Maybe they thought I had something to offer. When I was 17, I played in a Munster U-21 final against Kerry. They had Dara Ó Cinnéide and Darragh Ó Sé and all those guys – and they destroyed us. Ó Cinnéide hit about 1-9 that day. We hadn't a hope in hell but I loved it. I was playing for Paco and taking on Kerry in Fitzgerald Stadium. This was the 'big time'.

I actually ended up playing in three Munster finals at that grade and although, mentally, we were beaten before we went out, it was nice to reach that level.

After being in London for so long I had no expectations when I rejoined the Waterford set-up. In fact things were pretty much as I expected them to be. Player welfare was pretty poor and that annoyed me, but having just crawled into the dressing room I kept quiet for a while. Not too long, mind you. Maybe about three weeks.

Paul Ogle, Andy Heffernan and I shared a car journey from Tramore and the city to Dungarvan two or three times a week. We'd do some serious analysis and dissection in that car. We were always the first at training and the last out. We trained as hard as – if not harder than – anyone else. The thing I could never understand was why others didn't work as hard as us.

After a while the lads appointed me – or maybe I elected myself – the Gaelic Players' Association rep. I remember being nervous as hell before my first speech, standing up and telling the lads we were entitled to dinners, boots, gloves, training gear and all that.

Jesus, talk about the negativity.

All I got back from the floor was shite. One lad stood up and growled: 'New boots won't win you games'. Another fellow backed him up: 'Sure you have to win something to justify getting all that'.

I bit my lip.

Quite firmly, I told the boys that all these were things we were entitled to. I got thick enough about it; I asked how they expected others to respect them if they didn't respect themselves. All we wanted were warm showers – fuck it, even showers with a bit of water in them – a pair of free boots, a pair of gloves, the spot of dinner after games – these were all basic perks.

But there was resistance everywhere because lads felt we didn't deserve anything.

If you allow yourself to be treated shoddily, you will be.

We were getting tea or maybe soup and sandwiches after games. The gear? It might arrive and it might not.

There were times when we had no physio at games, no doctor and the food was shite. Poor Tom Condon had about 15 jobs. There were some evenings when I'd look around in training to see our goalkeeper Tom Wall coughing a lung up running 800-metre sprints with us when he should have been working with a goalkeeping coach. But we got on with it.

The main challenge was keeping that core group of lads together and Jackson has succeeded in doing that.

They were frustrating times; we didn't always play as consistently as we would have liked, but as the seasons passed we grew into a decent squad and a core friendship was built up.

Even now, I mightn't see lads for six months but I could lift the phone and take up from where we left off. The only regret I had taking the job as Wexford manager was that I couldn't play football for Waterford anymore. I'm still only 32 and if I could I'd still be with them.

The Cavan Conquest

Looking back, my happiest memory was the 2006 league game away to Cavan. I had a group of friends over from London for that game and one of them, Damien Keaney, was celebrating his 30th birthday. Jackson wanted us to drive up that morning, but I went the night before for the party. I drank water all night and went to bed at 11.30 p.m. but all I was hearing the whole night from the locals was: 'Take it handy on us tomorrow and go easy on us'.

A big sneer. They were chasing promotion at the time and they thought they would beat the living shite out of us. Even the landlord in my B&B was taking the Mick.

I went down to the field early that morning and remember seeing Tom Wall walking into the ground eating a Mars bar and glugging a can of Coke.

He had more sugar in him than the Siúcra factory in Thurles. The Cavan boys didn't know whether to laugh or cry. I wasn't sure what to do myself.

But in the dressing room we were totally relaxed. Because they were chasing promotion there was a huge crowd outside, while the only support we had was my gang over from London for the 30th birthday. There wasn't one native Waterford supporter at that game – I can say that with near certainty.

Out we went, stuck rigidly to the game plan and we beat them well. To this day, the London gang say it was the best game they ever saw, although they might be biased, I suppose.

But we actually played Cavan off the field and there was a stunned silence at the end. Afterwards, I had all my gear in the boot of the car and should have headed for home but I couldn't resist driving back out to the B&B to see the landlord.

I had no reason to go back out but I made one up. He didn't know where to turn when I arrived at the doorstep. He nearly fell over when he saw me. Mortified.

It was priceless.

After that, we believed that maybe, just maybe, we could mix it with the better teams. More importantly, we started to accept that we could play decent football. We picked off results more frequently. Slowly – morale lifted.

The big thing was that we all knew our roles. Mine was to withdraw from corner-forward and drop back to the middle of the field. I would have constantly shouted at lads throughout games and a lot of the lads would have been pissed off with me, but I think communication is a huge part of sport. I suppose I'd seen so much over the years, I felt I could bring something into the set-up.

We failed to get promotion during my time and we also failed to attract people to our games. Some days, with the Wexford job I have at the moment, I could be on the radio or interviewed by the press seven times a day. I think I was on the radio twice in five years in total with the Waterford team. There was no profile attached and very few wanted to know about it.

Even though a lot of things have now improved for the lads, there's still a lot of apathy out there. Please God they can change that because it's nice to know that your efforts are appreciated. I remember Ned English came in to coach us for one season and he gave every player in the squad a copy of the DVD Munster: The Road to Glory.

It was great to get it. I remember thinking that this man actually cares about us – he put a bit of thought into it. We were nearly misty at the eyes with that gesture.

Ned and I didn't always agree on my role with the team – he wanted us to be way more direct. But when you're at the bottom and you're clinging on, you don't want to leave yourself exposed. So we crowded our defence and broke from there. Ned wanted us to be more proactive but we preferred to soak up the pressure and break.

Other than that, I had a free hand really. Jackson just left me alone to get on with it.

In Search of the Golden Fleece

I was thinking back on my years with Waterford the other night and the first thing that struck me was that I never once swapped a jersey with an opponent after a game.

When I was a minor, our bus driver Mickey O'Shea asked us why anyone would exchange shirts with an opponent. Mickey maintained we worked hard enough to get it, so what was the point in giving it away?

I took a lot from that and kept every shirt. Even playing against the big boys, Cork and Kerry, I never went over and asked the superstars to swap. I burst my ass and was proud as hell to pull on the Waterford shirt. I wasn't going to hand it over.

People probably know me now as the Wexford football manager but there's a long story behind all that. And only for Waterford I wouldn't be where I am.

A lot of my current backroom team are from home; lads I can trust. The first call I made after getting the Wexford gig was to ring Michael Casey, a local physical trainer who had coached me at De La Salle. He tells me when I'm out of order, and when things are bad he reassures me. We [Wexford] had a serious season last year, reaching the All-Ireland semi-final. This year results have been poor but Michael and the rest are behind me.

People were shocked when I got the job but thanks to my 10 years in London, where I played senior championship hurling and football, and my time in Waterford, I had learned a lot about the lower end of the GAA. Every experience I had was worthwhile and I brought a lot of that to the Wexford job.

My time across the water was unreal. I taught PE at an Irish/Italian Catholic school in Chertsey, Surrey, where there were 1,700 students and six PE teachers. Physical education played a huge role in school life, with 240 minutes of devoted class time each week. At weekends we were still working, out looking after school teams. PE was handled in a very structured fashion.

It was fun too. To get full-time employment I had to acquire two things – a minibus driver's licence to ferry schoolkids around and a trampolining qualification. I kid you not. They wouldn't give me a job without both of those under my belt. So I got them and anything else they wanted I ticked the boxes. By the time I left I was head of the Sports Department in the school.

I'd studied teaching for four years in St Mary's, Strawberry Hill. I had started playing hurling with St Gabriels and Gaelic football with Tara, two local clubs. About a week before London were due to play Leitrim in the Connacht championship, I got a call to join their county squad. A call-up one week before a championship game!

We [London] struggled when the Celtic Tiger kicked off and people went back home although I do remember beating Limerick in the National Football League. That was like winning the All-Ireland final.

For a while, I thought I would never leave. But in 1997 I headed to the USA for the summer. I applied to the Major League Soccer franchise for work as a coach and was finally accepted after about four summers of trying.

I worked with the San Jose Earthquakes. One week I'd be helping a high-school team in a cup final, the next I'd be trying to win an U-12 state championship.

Soccer was a massive interest at the time and I was completely wrapped up in it during my time in California. Working for a franchise meant I could be farmed out anywhere and so every week I was in a new town, working with coaches from Crewe Alexandra and Newcastle United. I just soaked it all up.

At 27, I developed an urge to move back but I knew I wouldn't be able to leave London just like that. So I travelled the world for a year. Off I went to Tanzania, climbed Kilimanjaro, went skiing in New Zealand and settled in Sydney for a few months.

I met up with more Waterford lads there – Gary Hurney, John Phelan, Paul Maher and Tony Cormack – and we all ended up playing Gaelic football with Sydney. People criticise the GAA for different reasons but it was great to be able to keep fit and maintain that competitive edge whilst travelling.

Eventually the fun stopped. I came home. I got a job at Coláiste Cathal Naofa in Dungarvan in 2004 and met Suzanne Kavanagh around the same time. We married three years later and we have a little daughter, Aoibhe, now. Moving back proved to be a masterstroke.

Everything has just kind of fallen into place. I was proud to be a Waterford senior footballer for five years.

To be honest, I think I lived the dream.

Chapter 9
London Calling

Fear of Flying

13 March, Crown Plaza Hotel, Buckingham Gate, London.

Waterford's senior football players have reached London in a spirit of rare equanimity. Their desires are modest: a roof, a comfortable bed and some nourishing food. No need for red carpets or flowers in the lobby. A bit of grub and a night's sleep and they'll be ready to rumble.

They tiptoe wearily into the hotel just after 11 p.m. It's only a short hop from Cork Airport to Heathrow but some of them have been in transit since 10 a.m. For the likes of Sean Dempsey and John Hayden, students based in Dublin who had to travel to Cork Airport, the skip across the Irish Sea has turned into an odyssey.

Nonetheless, spirits are high. Most of the fun en route was had at the expense of Jackson, who clearly dreads flying – something to do with a bomb threat on a flight out of Darwin, Australia, about a decade ago. The players have dubbed him 'Mr T', in reference to the *A-Team* character who steadfastly refused to travel by air – and Jackson is every bit as rattled as the mohicaned one. The players don't quite have to inject him with tranquilisers to get him airborne, but his wife, Teresa, does slip him a sleeping tablet. By the time we pass through the gates he looks more relaxed than the cabin crew of Jamaica Airlines.

But the anxieties resurface as we climb towards the clouds. Nervously computing his chances of survival, he seeks reassurance from those nearest to him. He even taps the team's embedded correspondent on the shoulder.

'Hey, Lawlor, you must have been on loads of these,' he says with a glance around the cabin and a question in his voice.

'I have, Jackson. You're as safe as houses up here – safer than on the roads back home anyway.'

He seems temporarily reassured.

A few moments later, though, the confidence dips again. Conor McGrath is in the seat behind.

'Hey, McGrath, you must have been on loads of these before?'

'I have, Jackson.'

Teresa butts in. 'Will you relax, John, you'll be fine.'

Just then the plane hits an air pocket and a couple of speed bumps and starts to buck and groan. Jackson's face turns from a healthy red to a startled white and the colour drains further with every dip and wobble. His eyes are shut tighter than the Armagh defence on Ulster final day, but the lads don't spare him. As stomach-churning gusts of turbulence throw us from side to side they whoop in delight. Eventually we find calm air, and slowly relaxing his white-knuckle grip on the arm-rests, he regains an attitude of relative peace.

Some 50 minutes later we touch down. Jackson opens his eyes, leaps from his seat, punches the air with both fists and lets a roar of delight:

'LONDON, HERE I COME!'

The cabin erupts in laughter.

By now most passengers know there's a county football team on board. And when the captain comes on the PA to wish the boys luck, it's a rare buzz for a squad that could probably sneak unnoticed into Buckingham Palace and make off with the Queen herself.

It's an hour to the hotel, which actually turns out to be right next door to the Windsor family residence. As we check in, I discover that I'm paired with the team's First-Aid man, Michael Scanlon. We don't know each other from Adam but a budding friendship is almost immediately blighted as we enter the room to find there's only one bed.

Now, Michael, married with kids, is as safe as houses with me tucked in beside him, but the idea of sharing his bed – even a fine double one – with a red-blooded Tipperary man doesn't appeal to him. I'm not thrilled with the arrangement myself, but while I look for a diplomatic way to express reservations, Michael cuts to the chase.

'Oh, Jesus, we'll have to get this sorted out immediately,' he exclaims.

'You're right,' I say, greatly relieved.

We raise the mattress to see if it can somehow be split and, lo, we are greeted by two DVDs of a distinctly 'adult' genre. Like Holmes and Watson, we start speculating on the likely movements of the last guest. Perhaps he left in a rush. Or maybe his missus walked in and, panic-stricken, he thrust the offending items under the bed and later forgot about his stash. Anyway, the discovery has, if nothing else, broken the ice.

Paul Ogle, Liam Ó Líonáin and a few more hear the laughter from next door and charge in. We agree to give 'Debbie Does Dungarvan' an airing but insist on charging at the door. The lads offer to bring their own popcorn.

As we wait for our bed to be split into two, Michael, an academic and schoolteacher, explains how he got involved in the set-up. Jackson asked him to come on board last season and he's been with them since. He taught a number of the players in school and like everyone else he's hooked now.

Downstairs, the lads are hungry. Courtesy of the county board, they have €100 of spending money each, so it's a case of full pockets and empty stomachs. The problem is it's midnight. The hotel is far too posh to offer anything substantial at this late hour, and so they go looking for fast food. But this is the Queen's bailiwick; there ain't no Mackey Ds or Supermacs to be found. Within minutes they are back, ravenous but ready for bed.

They don't sleep particularly well either. Strange beds and all that. Yawning and stretching, they gather for breakfast the next morning. You can't imagine the Dublin or Tyrone superstars queueing like this for grub but some of the lads have to stand in line outside the dining-room for half an hour. There are no tantrums, though, and along with the other guests they patiently join the tailback.

Told to meet in the lobby at 10.30 a.m., they convene for a meeting but it turns out to be only a brief discussion of the travel arrangements to Ruislip. Some of the players are less than impressed; they still don't know the starting 15 and wanted a chat to get focused. It doesn't happen.

They ramble around the neighbourhood to pass the time. At midday, a little tetchy, they embark on the journey to the ground.

Their playmaker Liam Lawlor is marked absent today and his teammates are, to say the least, disappointed. Lawlor has long since flagged the fact he has a thesis to hand in this weekend but his teammates need him and feel he should be here.

Meanwhile, those picked to play have already been informed. Ogle and John Phelan have been told they are on the bench.

The Lost Bus

On the way to Ruislip the bus gets lost. Thankfully, we have some time in hand, but the driver, not from these parts, is totally innocent as to the location of the stadium.

He finds Ruislip Road and thinks he's on the right track, but that's like hitting Limerick Junction and thinking you're in Limerick.

A quick call to Tommy Harrell, the London GAA chairman, confirms what we suspect. Like a Fianna Fáil budgetary estimate, we're all at sea with a dodgy compass.

'Excuse me, mate,' the driver shouts out the window to one bemused motorist.

'Where's the football ground?'

The motorist starts describing the quickest way to Wembley, until one of the players runs up to our driver and informs him that we're not here to play soccer.

'We're a GAA team,' he explains.

'You what?'

There's no time to explain. By now Phileas Fogg is animated, perplexed and perspiring heavily. There's a long mile of traffic ahead of us and it doesn't help that we're actually going the wrong way. Worse still, there's nowhere to do a U-turn.

Time to execute Plan B.

'Excuse me, mate,' Fogg roars to another slow-moving motorist.

'By any chance do you know where the GEE-AYE-AYE football ground is?'

Clearly suspecting that our man is a few pennies short of a full pound sterling, the fellow lets on not to hear – from two yards away, with his window down.

Patience is wearing thin. Cian O'Connor, the physio, does a Chris Tarrant and phones a friend, who finally sets Fogg straight. We're to take the A40 and turn off at the Polish War Memorial.

But no, Phileas has other ideas. He's got this far by his own orienteering skills and he's not for turning now. The memorial yawns in front of our eyes and the whole bus roars at him to go for it, but just as the goalmouth opens before us we trickle harmlessly wide and take a slip road left. Cue more groans from the terraces.

'It's okay, mate, I couldn't go straight because the cops were up there but I know where I'm going now.'

In other words, this joker probably doesn't have a driver's licence. But then we see a Tricolour waving in the wind and it's like the first shaft of sunlight after a storm.

Either this is Ruislip or the English are really buying into St Patrick's Day.

We pull into the grounds and it's as we expected: sandy pitch, clubhouse, nice and compact. The players hop off the bus and a clearly-relieved Fogg throws the gear and luggage off with renewed zest. There's 90 minutes to throw-in and some of the team go for a kick-around as the rest head into the clubhouse to watch Liverpool pummel Manchester United 4-1.

This time last year Waterford hammered a mostly English-born London side, but a glance around the bar suggests there will be no annihilation this time. The 2009 outfit is a powerful one, with men from several corners of Ireland – Tyrone, Galway, Cork and Longford included.

To date they have lost narrowly to Sligo, Antrim and Leitrim and today they have targeted a win. Waterford are well within their range. Their manager, Noel Dunning, has gone on record to that effect.

Worryingly, there's a sense of lethargy about Kiely's men, many of whom are hungry, having not eaten since nine in the morning. One or two buy peanuts and snacks in the clubhouse bar before they tog out. There are a few bags of potato crisps consumed as well. The sports nutritionists would cringe.

It doesn't help either that while some are upstairs watching the soccer, others are on the field playing headers and volleys. You can imagine how the London camp might use that for motivation.

At 2.40 p.m. the team is announced for the first time and in the dressing room McLoughlin lays it on the line.

'Today, you are set up for a kick in the bollocks,' he states with the certainty of a man who knows something of the excruciating pain entailed.

'All this year we've been going well, but today you are ripe for that kick. They feel they can beat you. They have footballers from strong counties all over Ireland and they don't fear you in the slightest. To them, you're small fry. It's up to you to show that we have great footballers in Waterford too.'

McLoughlin emphasises that all around the ground there's a sense of an upset in the air.

'Unless you are fully committed and hungry for everything, you're in trouble today,' he says. 'To win, you'll have to play with intensity. If you don't, we're gone. Lads, you can see for yourselves, they think they'll beat us.'

Kiely takes the floor and explains that Ger Power will fill the quarter-back role in place of the exam-tied Lawlor. The three O'Gorman lads have made the journey over after the untimely death of their father and two of them, Thomas and Maurice, go straight into the team. As they take the field, they can clearly see the London side are up for it.

Led by Martin McGrath, the former Mayo trainer who helped the county reach the 2006 All-Ireland final, they race past cones and hammer into each other in the warm-up. They do their work outside the pitch and two mantras are audible from McGrath's pep talk: 'Two points' and 'Intensity.'

The referee, Eddie Craul of Wicklow, calls the captains together and the game gets underway. Two things are noticeable right from the start; Waterford are absolutely dire and Craul's decisions are going against them. Several frees awarded against Kiely's men are, to put it mildly, surprising and allow the home team to take an early grasp on the game.

Waterford miss numerous point chances. When they do get the odd free, their radar is no better than that of our old friend Phileas Fogg. Today they would struggle to hit the proverbial cow's arse with a banjo.

This is the side of Waterford football the players had told me about. A dark side that sometimes emerges when they are flagged to win a game. There's no explaining it.

They could go out a week later and run Kerry to six points but when something is expected of them they are liable to implode.

That's what's happening here. Paul Geraghty, who used to play midfield for the Galway seniors, is lording it for London in the centre of the pitch. Apart from Mick Ahearne's industry, Kiely's men have no answer.

Lawlor's calm passing and intelligent link-play are hugely missed. They have plenty of possession but there's no end product. In contrast, Chris Donnellan, brother of Michael, the two-time Tribesmen All-Ireland medal winner, dominates at full-forward. The Exiles lead 0-7 to 0-5 at the break.

Inside, McLoughlin loses the rag. And you can't blame him.

'Do ye want to go back to how ye used to be?' he roars. 'Do ye really want that? Because if we lose this game that's where we're fucking headed! Ye decide!'

The players are furious with themselves too, but there's way too much shouting in the dressing room. It feels like panic stations.

No matter what way they dress it up, complacency has set in; the preparation was terrible and they've been caught on the hop. At the top level, teams can ship a bad half-hour and still resurface and turn it on, but when you're Waterford, any little setback is magnified. Self-doubt spreads like a rash. A good run can begin to unravel with a few points conceded – and that's what's happening here.

They go out and proceed to control the second half but miss chance after chance, free after free. Stephen Cunningham comes on and makes an instant impression but hasn't enough time to make a telling dent. Worse still, their main man, Ó Líonáin, has been struggling with an injury from the start and should not even be on the field. But they need him; even on one leg he's likely to raise a flag. The gamble fails, however. They lose by a point: 0-9 to 0-8.

Utter, unmitigated, sickening disaster.

A Laughing Stock

It knocks the stuffing out of everyone. The brief euphoria over recent achievements has been brutally punctured. Tonight in London will be horrendous. The trip was supposed to be a mini-break, a reward for their League heroics to date. But everyone involved took their eye off the ball. Their night on the town will be a write-off.

Back in the dressing room, no one speaks. Brian Wall, who uncharacteristically missed a heap of frees, is inconsolable – so distraught he actually throws up.

The management team are speechless. To twist the knife, London didn't even crack loose at the final whistle. They clenched fists and the players hit each other a thump of appreciation as they walk off. But it was clear they fully expected to win.

Tom Wall tries to make sense of it all and eventually asks for a few minutes before summing it up succinctly.

'I've lost five county finals in hurling and football over the past couple of years. I've been on teams that were hammered by Cork and Kerry in the championship. But that is as low as I've ever been. I've had seven years with this team but this is fucking cruel,' he says softly, his face visibly etched with the pain of it all.

Amazingly, Wall hasn't let in a goal since the team lost to Kerry in the 2007 Munster championship, and he's at a loss to know how his side have been beaten by London. In the end, he blames a lack of concentration.

'I think too many lads were looking ahead to the weekend away and thinking about the Saturday night on the town,' he muses. 'We should have flown in this morning and flown home tonight. But if that happened we'd be moaning about not getting a weekend away. We never get a thing so we were all looking forward to this. But we took our eye off the ball. We have to clear the air now – a lot of things went wrong, on the side of management as well as players.'

Wall is right. There were sinful errors made by a number of individuals, especially in front of the posts, but football is primarily a collective endeavour, and the art of screwing up spectacularly is not confined to individuals. All have to admit their guilt.

The mood on the bus back to the hotel is dark; half the squad want to get out of London right away. Players underperformed, some were played out of position and their final pass killed them time and again. Now they're fighting an uphill battle to get out of the slums.

A day later, Antrim and Sligo both win, leaving Waterford in fourth place, three points behind but with games against Leitrim, Carlow, Antrim and Sligo to come. After losing to London they are cannon fodder again.

It's not just the team and management that the result has affected. I've been with these lads for nearly five months now and whether I like it or not I'm part of them. They've gone out of their way to help me record their season, given their time freely and greeted me like a brother at every game and training session. I consider them friends.

Duty calls and I have to leave London early to go back to the day job. Tommy Harrell drops me to Heathrow Airport.

My own weekend has been ruined and in the following days I am forced to the conclusion that they've missed the boat. It's a lousy feeling to see guys who have trained so honestly and tried so bloody hard to get out of where they are get sucker-punched like this.

Still, the writing had been on the wall. Since the Wicklow game they've gone backwards in attack, crowded out by opposing defences. Their own defence is fine, but it's clear that their off-the-ball running has deteriorated over the season – therefore defenders can handle them quite easily. Their final pass and shooting in front of the posts continue to let them down – they struggle to kick accurately from 30 yards out. Half the counties in Ireland have that problem but some of them can boast at least one clinical corner-forward to get them out of jail. Waterford cannot.

Two days later, Wall has had more time to gather his thoughts.

'A players' meeting is required to clear the air,' he states. 'I'll be looking for one anyway. It's like this, if we don't beat Leitrim I think our season could be over. By that I mean that lads will go back training with their clubs rather than their county again and they'll not give a shit about what we're trying to do.

'It's totally frustrating. I went back home on Sunday night and got some slagging off the locals. We were a laughing stock again. I hate that. Lads calling me all day Monday, having a pop. Sickening. And they laughing at us.'

Other players recounted the reactions they had faced in various places in the days that followed. John Hayden, dressed in the team's training gear, went for a run the day after they flew home and car after car honked horns at him. One guy slowed, let the window down, asked if the Queen was happy London had won and drove off laughing heartily.

'Sure you could see people pointing at us when we flew back into Cork Airport. You don't have to be a genius to know what they were saying. There's Waterford. London beat them yesterday.'

There was indeed plenty of sniggering among bystanders as the team grabbed their bags from the carousel in Cork Airport, and one punter couldn't resist a more vocal pop at the team.

'Jesus, lads, what were ye doing? Beaten by London!' he said for the full benefit of friends and bystanders.

Most of the players ignored the jibe. But one of the lads had an answer. From somewhere at the back of the group came the riposte loud and clear.

'Sure what the fuck did you expect? Don't they have the pick of 10 million people.'

Bad and all as the weekend was, you could only laugh.

Chapter 10
The Underdogs

Back to Basics
——•——

10 a.m., 17 March, Lemybrien, County Waterford

They can still hear the music but you can't help wondering if Waterford's dance is over for another year.

There's much soul-searching to be done and on the way back from London the players waste no time in turning the spotlight on themselves. They ask to train at 10 a.m. on St Patrick's Day. Many of them have family commitments and 101 other things to be doing but they've taken it upon themselves to get back to the training ground and rectify the glaring problems the cross-channel trip has revealed.

Traditionally, their enigma value has increased as mediocre results were sandwiched between the odd big scalp. But these players are hankering after steadiness. Back to the field. Time to roll the dice again.

It's a two-hour session and it's good. There's a real sense of urgency. They warm up and quickly ask for an internal match to get the weekend out of their system. They need it.

At half-time they huddle together and Maurice O'Gorman calls for more intensity.

'Lads, we have to make tougher hits in games,' he says. 'We have to be colder and start intimidating teams. Not one of us made a decent hit against London and we didn't make anyone think twice about tackling us either. We're too nice.'

The ball is rolling now and players are quick to respond. One by one they step up and express their angst, articulating a catalogue of problems. It's like a group-therapy session.

The trip was a farce. No team talk. They didn't know the line-up until 30 minutes before throw-in. No pre-match meal. Players eating crisps an hour before the game.

Players watching Premiership soccer minutes beforehand. Lads too focused on going on the piss for the weekend.

As the players hold a mirror to themselves, the management take a good look at their reflection too.

They should have held a tighter rein on the team. There's too much clutter on the sideline, not enough real communication. The morning of the game, half the backroom wanted a team meeting in the hotel and the other half didn't. In hindsight it was badly needed.

Today, the management are listening to the players, who want the O'Gormans back in their rightful berths on the full-back line. A team can be built from there. Up to now the O'Gormans have been used to plug holes wherever they appeared. You can't blame Jackson for that; those sinewy twins could play anywhere. But for now they are needed at the back to steady the ship.

Maurice appreciates the manager's logic in employing their running ability farther upfield, but ultimately they are defenders, man-markers. They want to go back to what they know best.

Kiely is now inclined to agree. His defence has been motoring well but has been loose at times – the twins' tenacity is needed there again. He tells Maurice O'Gorman they'll be back where they belong for the Leitrim match. In turn he wants to hear more from him in the dressing room; as a captain he's too quiet. Time to lead by words as well as action. This team badly needs a lift from somewhere or else it's curtains.

All the issues are taken on board but there's no finger-pointing, no blame game. They've been through too much for that. They all shoulder some responsibility for what went wrong. They end with a round of applause and hit the showers, hoping to wash away the lingering odours of a lost weekend in London.

They train again on Friday and ask for another chat afterwards. Kiely duly calls on Maurice O'Gorman, Mick Ahearne and Brian Wall – three key players but gentle fellows – to address the team.

The captain is first up and lets Liam Lawlor have it over missing the London game.

The exam-blitzed Lawlor has received a frosty enough reception from teammates, but at least now it's all out in the open, which is healthy. There's no backstabbing; what needs to be said is said.

The general tone of this meeting is redemption. The team to play Leitrim is picked and players know where they stand. Ahearne misses out because of a problem with an AC joint and so Brian Wall moves to midfield. The O'Gormans are at home in the full-back line. Shane Briggs is fully recovered from his cruciate and comes in at centre-back. Eddie Rockett moves to the wing and Lawlor comes back as sweeper.

It's a strong side. Players leave the dressing room that evening knowing two more points are up for grabs. If they can get their paws on them it's 'game on' again.

In days gone by, Waterford would have imploded after losing to London but the current model is more resilient. After two clear-the-air sessions and a series of tweaks, the engine is oiled and raring for road once more. Spirits are raised again. Amazing what a few days can do.

Before they leave Lemybrien, Kiely reminds them that it's been a good week but now is the time to do their talking on the field.

'Ye're underdogs again,' he says. 'A fucking laughing stock after last weekend. People in your own county are as bad as anywhere else with the mocking. It's up to ye to get us back again.'

Heads nod furiously in agreement. This time they leave the training base with spears sharpened, well prepared and ready for battle. Sometimes in sport it's the attention to detail before games that makes all the difference. Scrap that. It's the attention to detail all the time.

The Visit of Leitrim

22 March, Fraher Field, County Waterford. NFL Round 5 v Leitrim

THAT well-travelled double act, Mickey Moran and John Morrison, take the Leitrim team through their warm-up and link arms with their latest group of players. In days of yore the old sages have worked their magic with Mayo and Derry. They are now trying to conjure miracles with the Connacht minnows. After they finish speaking, a huge roar erupts from the team circle and, wired with headsets and portable microphones, Moran makes his way to the dug-out. It seems the modern manager must look like a 2FM disc jockey – Jackson is clearly lagging behind the times.

He's too country 'n' western for that craic.

Under Moran's watch, little is left to chance, and Leitrim duly travelled south last night and stayed over. On a high from beating Wicklow the week before, they are two points ahead of Kiely's men in the table. Another win this afternoon will leave them poised to reach Division 3.

In contrast to the 20 or so locals in attendance, they've brought a couple of hundred supporters with them. From start to finish these diehards are extremely vocal. Everything looks smooth for them.

But in the Waterford dressing room players are far more focused than the weekend before. It's sink-or-swim time. The bookies have them at 2 to 1 to win. They're written off again and, yes, that suits just fine.

Kiely ups the ante and at the same time throws down the gauntlet. The less cuddly side of him has been on view these past few days and it's more striking.

'Ye've done the talking. Now go out there and back it up,' he challenges the team.

'Ye probably think I'm mad in the head but I'm telling you straight that we have the better footballers – we're way better than them. But they're cocksure that they'll turn us over. They have big-name managers and all the rest and they think the big-time is only around the corner.

'What the fuck have we lads? At the moment we have nothing only the fucking jersey we're playing for. Our pride took a fierce battering last week but that was only a blip.

'Show me now it was only a blip. We have our best possible team out today. It's over to ye now.'

Out they sprint onto the field to warm up.

It's been a sensational weekend for Irish sport. Just 24 hours earlier the rugby team won the Grand Slam in sensational style. On Saturday night Bernard Dunne snatched the World WBA superbantamweight title in an epic bout at the O2 arena. The weather is tremendous and after catching a breath of spring the country is buzzing.

But here and now, in the forgotten hinterland of Division 4, this is the only game that counts. The exalted feats of the previous day are forgotten as Waterford and Leitrim go head to head in their own battle, far from the media glare and the frenetic roars of the masses. No one outside of here gives a tinker's curse about what happens on this pitch today; Monday's papers will give it a cursory three or four paragraphs. But in the two camps those involved are straining every sinew to land a precious win.

Clad in fresh green and gold shirts the visitors start off like world-beaters. They feed the ball crisply into the corner channels and their corner-forwards sprint in the opposite direction, taking Mark Prendergast and Maurice O'Gorman with them and leaving acres of space for their full-forward Declan Maxwell to dash into. Maxwell duly pops over a lovely early point and straightaway Waterford heads drop.

For the next few minutes they seem to be chasing shadows. Leitrim are playing to a plan and Kiely's men are all over the place, pulled hither and tither and made to look inept.

But Leitrim are not in the bottom tier without reason. Their shooting turns out to be desperately poor and Waterford take heart from the fact that they miss chance after chance to score.

It takes Waterford a while to settle but eventually they find their feet. Liam Lawlor has a point to prove. He starts stringing the passes together and coaxing teammates into their rhythm. Three quick handpasses send Liam Ó Líonáin on his way to goal but he blasts it wide. In recent weeks, the forwards coach Colin Kelly has been advising Ó Líonáin to pass the ball to the net, not just blast it. It seems the advice has gone unheeded.

Moments later, though, he's on his way again, blazing down the right flank, cutting in. This time, remembering Kelly's counsel, he places a superb goal. He does the same thing again five minutes after, stretching the net after taking on three Leitrim defenders. If the Gooch had scored these goals we'd be kneeling at his altar for weeks, but here only 234 spectators have assembled to witness Ó Líonáin's double strike. At least Kiely appreciates his genius.

'I've been dreaming of Liam Ó doing that for the past two years,' he says, smiling like a proud father on the sideline. 'And the dreams have come true. They were the perfect goals.'

Today, Kiely has Tom Condon and Ger Power nearby for support. Paul McLoughlin is in the stands armed with a mobile phone and Mick O'Loughlin has taken shelter at the opposite side of the pitch. On the touchline there's more space and less agitation.

It works.

Against the breeze, Waterford are suddenly six points up. The Leitrim sideline are left scratching their heads but it isn't rocket science – their players cannot live with Ó Líonáin's lightning forays into their territory.

Ó Líonáin is way better than he actually thinks he is. All year long he has beaten opponents with his pace, cutting through defences with glorious menace. Sometimes he shoots with too much power and the ball roars wide. They want to get more accuracy out of him. But he's a gem.

One evening in training Colin Kelly called him aside. He was wearing a Munster interprovincial shirt and Kelly enquired where he got it.

'I was picked on the panel last year,' Ó Líonáin replied meekly.

Kelly knew that.

'Well, it's about time you started believing it's yours,' he told the young schoolteacher. 'You got that shirt on merit. They don't hand them out for fun.'

Bit by bit he's starting to understand that he can do incredible things with the ball. He has blistering speed and if he cultivates more poise he can be the best forward in the division. His teammates know as much.

Today his two goals have motivated them. Seán O'Hare, after a few below-par displays, is on fire. Wayne Hennessy, another talent at left wing-back, is having the game of his life.

On the sideline the Leitrim mentors, Moran and Morrison, look agitated. They weren't expecting this.

Flustered, they summon their star man, Emelyn Mulligan, who is struggling with shingles, from the bench and detail a marker to follow Lawlor. They also whip off their entire full-forward line by half-time. Thanks to the breeze and Mulligan, they claw their way back and at the interval they trail by only two points. It was never going to be easy for Waterford.

The half-time speeches are short and to the point. Paul McLoughlin: 'You're well on top. Just stop soloing the ball into contact, cut out the silly frees, keep the scoreboard ticking over and this game is in the bag.'

Ó Líonáin has had to go off with a quad-muscle strain during the first half but the manager tells the team he's ready to come back on if needed. That lifts them – a safety net, if you like.

Then Kiely looks at Eddie Rockett, now on the wing and having his first bad game of the year.

'Eddie, if you're a gambler and you back a horse to win and at the end the jockey falls, what do you do?' Kiely asks.

He supplies the answer before Eddie gets a chance to respond. 'You back him to get on the horse again and look to the next race.'

'Because you believe in him. I'm backing you to get on the horse again.'

It's positive all the way. You can tell from the mood that Waterford are going to hang on here. It's that type of afternoon.

Leitrim get the first score on the resumption but are exposed whenever the home team attacks. When the tempo drops, Tony Grey, a real impact sub, comes off the bench to liven things up. After a series of quick passes he finds Hennessy, who posts a sublime point on the run from 40 yards with the right foot. It arcs beautifully in the breeze and in fact has no place in an occasion like this; it's a Division One score.

They're awarded a penalty soon after and Thomas O'Gorman struts up from full-back to apply the finishing touch. It isn't the greatest of penalty kicks – 'manky' is one description – but it gets there.

Leitrim snatch a late goal, the first Tom Wall has conceded since 1937 or so it seems, but it makes no difference. Waterford win by three, 3-7 to 1-10. Season still alive.

It's taken sheer guts for the minnows to respond.

In the dressing room Kiely lauds his men for showing the Irish version of cojones – *liathróidí*. They didn't wipe the floor with the opposition but they were hungrier.

Long after the game has ended Mickey Moran and John Morrison are chatting in the dressing room, disappointed at how their team has played. Two members of Kiely's camp pop in and ask what they thought of the game. They also asked Moran and Morrison what they thought of Waterford and how the Waterford management could improve their side.

'I was really honoured by that,' Morrison says. 'Those lads just want to learn, they are honest and all they want is for their team to improve. I admire that big-time. If I'm being honest, I told them we had our chances

124

to win and that they retreated a bit near the end of the game. But I'm starting to understand where they are coming from. I'm starting to learn how people think at this level.'

People were astonished when the Moran/Morrison double act arrived in Leitrim after high-profile gigs with Donegal, Mayo and Derry. They are hugely respected, and Morrison, especially, is known for his unique approach. As Mayo coach he sent the entire squad a Valentine's Day card to show them how much he cared. Now the double act is with Leitrim. It's not a match-up many would have expected but John gets a little miffed when asked to explain the move.

'The simple answer is because we were asked and because Leitrim were persistent about it. And now we're here it's all about changing the mindset. These guys are almost expecting failure; they don't know to expect anything else. Since we came in we have been raising standards and hopefully they'll learn from it. I'm not being big-headed or anything but we have come from a Division One base and you take things for granted.'

Like proper preparation for example.

'We urine-tested the lads the Thursday night before we played Waterford and every one of them was properly hydrated. But the five-hour journey down here took a lot out of them and the night before the game most of them were dehydrated. We tried to encourage them to drink two pints of water but then a lot of them were up in the middle of the night, in a strange bed, restless. By the time the game came around not one of the players was hydrated. No wonder they were so sluggish at the start. They were dead on their feet and Waterford struck for two goals. End of game.

'People will think we must be killing them in training. Not at all – everything we do is sharp and around the ball. What really happened was they didn't prepare well and we suffered. But Mickey and I will learn from that. Any player who isn't hydrated by the middle of next week won't be in our match panel next weekend against Kilkenny.

'The worst thing about it was that there wasn't even a bottle of water to be had on the bus journey back home. But we know we're dealing with limited resources and we can't push it – we have to introduce things one at a time.'

So far this season the smallest number at a Leitrim training session has been 34; in previous years Leitrim would have found it hard to get 34 for their championship panel. Before each session, a sheet is pinned on the wall describing the schedule ahead, underlining the main aspects of it and informing the players what they will learn from it. After every match, Morrison gets his players to rate themselves and he puts them in three boxes: Thriving, Surviving and Diving. The results have been telling.

'What's apparent is that most of the players have underrated themselves. So I've had to get involved and get them to point out the positive things they have done over the past seven days and then see how they can address the negatives. Gradually they are becoming more comfortable with rating themselves highly.

'We are making progress all the time but it won't happen overnight. Like, a few weeks back, I read Pat Spillane's column. After one defeat he wrote that he expected more from a team coached by Mickey Moran and John Morrison. I rang him to say I was disappointed with that. He asked why and I replied: "Pat, if you wrote something like that after we had been with them for three years I would have no complaints but we're only with the lads four months. What do you expect?"

'People have to lay off. Teams are very fragile in Division 4. We are working on changing the mindsets. That's the biggest challenge. But I'll tell you one thing – if we can achieve success during our time here it will be sweeter than any of the triumphs we've experienced in our coaching careers.'

The Leitrim bus pulls away and heads north-west. Reports later indicate that there's scarcely a word uttered on the coach as they make their way home. Another team has been 'Jacksoned'.

The failure of the Leitrim players to stay hydrated is another indication of the happy-go-lucky approach of teams at this level. Other glitches include loss of concentration, players taking holidays during the season, taking match days off and not warming up properly. Then they wonder why results don't go their way.

What happened to Waterford in London is very similar to what happened to Leitrim in Fraher Field. One aspect of their pre-match preparation was way off and they lost by three points.

But the Waterford backroom team seem utterly determined that such apathy won't creep in again. A day after their latest win a text arrives from Mick O'Loughlin. The Leitrim game isn't even mentioned. It reads: 'Training Monday and Wednesday and another session/team meeting on Friday night. All focus on Carlow now. Carlow, Carlow, Carlow. Nothing else.'

Three sessions and a chat – that's two gatherings more than they had the week before they played the Exiles. They may be learning the hard way but at least they're learning.

Carlow Come Calling

2.30 p.m., 28 March, Fraher Field, County Waterford.
NFL Round 6 v Carlow

There's something in the air and it don't smell rosy. It's called doubt and negativity.

The players are visibly weighed down with worry. The dressing room is full of fear, a dark room where negatives are developed.

It doesn't help that Ó Líonáin is injured and out of commission. Against Leitrim they had to do without Mick Ahearne but today they are minus the services of their top scorer, their leading attacker. For the past few weeks he's been struggling to shake off a quad injury and he's just not able to start. They hand him the number 24 jersey and tell him to keep warm throughout the game: 'We might need you yet'. How prophetic those words prove to be!

127

Carlow are in town. As usual, their best players are unavailable for all the old reasons, club loyalties and the like. And many of those who did link up with the squad at the start of the season have since pulled out. In recent years they've done themselves no favours at all with their club-versus-county civil wars and their general indifference toward the tri-coloured shirt.

Before the game their manager, Luke Dempsey, shows Jackson a couple of text messages he got from players notifying him of their withdrawals. Kiely, however, looks at the dates of the texts and sees they are several weeks old. Dempsey is trying to lure our man into a state of overconfidence but no one is fooled. Those Carlow players he's referring to are gone a long time.

The game starts and the visitors do everything bar park the team bus across their defence. They do a Waterford on it and plant 12 men behind the ball, with two left in the full-forward line and one on the half-forward line. The rest break up play and fire the ball quickly up the field. It works a treat in the opening 10 minutes; they win three frees and Johnny Kavanagh effortlessly points them.

It's exactly like the London game; Waterford own the ball but can't find a score.

Without Ó Líonáin they are bereft of pace and ideas. It's miserable to watch. At the break Carlow lead 0-5 to 0-3. McLoughlin and Kiely lose the cool.

'What the fuck was that?' McLoughlin asks. 'Three times this year teams have put it up to ye and ye haven't responded. UL put it up to ye and ye faded. London put it up to ye and ye wilted too. And today Carlow are putting it up to ye and what do ye respond with? A whimper. Today is about two points. Are ye going to let them walk all over ye, for Christ's sake? If ye are, forget about it.'

He turns away. He's furious.

Kiely takes the floor and addresses Michael O'Gorman, who started at

128

full-forward but has seen nothing of the ball.

'Michael, we're taking you off. I'm sorry. I know the style out there doesn't suit you but we have to do something.'

He turns to Ó Líonáin.

'Liam you're coming on and going in full-forward. And make no mistake, Liam, you're coming on to win the fucking game for us.'

The players are left alone to gather their thoughts. By now, the anxiety that was there before the game has worked its way down the production line and has been boxed into frustration. They need a response. Quickly.

Ogle answers the call. He races out of defence to point in the 42nd minute but it's another 18 minutes before the scores are level as both teams dish up a shocking travesty of the art of shooting. Then, with seven minutes left, Ó Líonáin strikes for a crucial goal. Shane Briggs and Cillian O'Keeffe add scores. Waterford hang on to win 1-7 to 0-6. It hasn't been pretty but the points are in the bag.

Later that night Antrim hammer Sligo, which means Waterford have to beat Sligo away from home to have any chance of promotion. And they'll have to beat Antrim after that. Two cup finals to get to Division 3; that's what faces them now.

'We can still do it,' Ó Líonáin says as he changes back into his street clothes.

'I think we'll raise it against Sligo. We always play better against the more high-profile counties and we always play better away from home – for some reason.'

The 24-year-old is single-handedly carrying the team at the moment. He won a provincial U-21 title in 2003 but he's the only member of that team on the senior squad. Where else would you see it? An entire underage team wiped out of senior contention within six years.

This guy is only getting better though. He has played twice for the Munster interprovincial side over the past four seasons, and his ability has never been in doubt, but this season the Ring clubman is the vital cog. He's

129

scored 6-7 from play so far and of the frees that Brian Wall has pointed, 18 have come from direct fouls on Ó Líonáin.

There are times when it seems the pressure is getting to him but today's goal was class – a rocket to the net from 14 yards out.

There are times when he revels in the responsibility too.

'A bit of experience helps,' he nods. 'I have a lot to prove and it would be just great to get out of where we are. We need to change the perception surrounding Waterford football. Even when I went playing for Munster, people wouldn't give you a second look because you were a Waterford footballer.

'When I was called up first three years back, I was hoping for a run against Leinster but they brought on a Cork sub instead. I was a regular Waterford starter at the time but this guy they brought on was only a sub with Cork. That's what they thought of me,' he chuckles softly.

'Then I got a start last season but they took me off and brought on a Cork U-21 player so maybe I'm not as good as I think I am,' he adds, still laughing.

'I'm enjoying the year though. It's the first time in ages I've been able to get a good run without serious injury. I get the ball and take off. While I have a bit of speed I might as well use it. I'm still not taking all my chances though; I have a tendency to shoot hard and fast. But when you're in full flight and bearing down on goal it's hard to think of everything.'

Two Hurlers Needed

Two nights later the team assemble for training but it's just a yoga session and some light stretching. Mel Shanley visits them the following Wednesday to go through some strength-and-conditioning routines. At this stage Kiely's backroom are trying to keep things fresh.

They discuss the possibility of bringing in a high-profile manager to talk to them and an approach is made to Mickey Harte. He willingly agrees to give up his time and address the team on the following Saturday, 4 April.

He says he will meet the team at the Citywest Hotel near Dublin around lunchtime. Kiely is delighted and puts the proposal to the board. But his request is turned down due to the cost of sending a team to Dublin and paying for 30 meals.

In the current climate the decision is understandable but when you look back at 2008 it's hard to credit too. In that year the county board spent over €500,000 on the senior hurlers, but now they won't pay to send the footballers to Dublin for a talk by Mickey Harte.

Still, Jackson refuses to rant and rave.

'There are good men on that board,' he says diplomatically, 'the money just isn't there. It's a pity because Mickey would give any man in this country good advice and it would have sharpened us up no end. I think we're gone a little stale, mentally.

'We've been hyping the lads up week after week for certain games but it's draining, and a chat with the likes of Mickey Harte would have worked wonders. But sure it's not to be.'

But the GAA takes and the GAA gives and it's not all bad news. Unprompted, the county board contact Davy Fitzgerald and ask him to make Gary Hurney available for the last two league games, or the Sligo game at the very least. The hurlers are out of contention for the Division One title and the board realise Hurney is badly needed on the football team.

In fact that's an understatement. Without him, the ball cannot stick up front and most of the players are so unsure of themselves they are trying to walk the ball into the net or fist it over – they're that terrified of shooting. Hurney could be the missing catalyst.

It's agreed to name him at number 27 on the programme for the Sligo match. He will start at full-forward instead of the injured Sean Fleming.

The reaction of the rest of the players who have been training all year will be interesting but Kiely has already decided he needs the big man. No matter what the others say he's coming back for the next game.

Most of the players are ready to welcome him back with open arms but there will be one or two dissidents. There always are.

'The way I see it,' Ó Líonáin argues, 'Gary has given 10 years of his life to playing football for Waterford. He's taken a chance to join the hurlers in the past year or two and who could blame him. But we are struggling without him, I don't know how many times I have thought about him after matches, so I would be delighted to see him back.'

One or two players have already approached Kiely to say they're willing to step down from the first 15 in order to get Hurney back. In training, the manager doesn't confirm or deny that the big man is returning but after a meeting with his selectors they decide to reinstall him. He's left out of the match programme altogether and the development is kept from the media. What Sligo don't know won't hurt them.

After training, the players are told that a team including Seán Fleming and Stephen Cunningham has been named and released to the press, but the players are to disregard it – it's a dummy selection; a different 15 will line out. Cunningham has joined Fleming on the injury list so neither will be selected.

It transpires that Shane Walsh, another hurler, will join Hurney in returning to the football squad.

Most of the incumbents are happy with developments, but one or two of the fringe players and panellists who were hoping for a promotion are wondering what they're making all the effort for.

'Will they be with us for the rest of the year and train every night with us?' asks the centre-back Shane Briggs.

Jackson is unrelenting: 'They've given great service to Waterford football over the years. We're short two forwards, we're struggling for scores and we need to win the game. They are helping us out. But they are on the hurling panel. So they won't be with us for the whole year. Our aim is to get promotion; that would be like an All-Ireland title for us. If they can help us to achieve that, so be it.'

Briggs is good friends with Hurney – they are clubmates – and he's guaranteed his place. But it doesn't stop him seeking reassurance that Hurney will stay with them beyond the Sligo game.

'I want to get up to Division 3 as much as the next fella,' Briggs reasons after the meeting, 'and I know Gary will be a big shove-on. I'm good friends with him and I rate him highly as a footballer and as a lad. But it's no use that he and Shane come and go. We need them training with us and playing the rest of the games.

'It's okay for me – I'm back on the team – but what about the subs? What hope have they of getting a game when they see the two boys coming back and walking straight in? There's a bigger issue here, I have no problem with Gary hurling – he deserves it. But he wants to play football too and something should be arranged to help him do that.'

Before they head for home, the players are reminded to say nothing about the return of Hurney and Walsh; it's intended as an unpleasant surprise for Sligo.

After the weights session with Shanley, they move on to get some grub and watch the closing stages of Ireland and Italy in the World Cup qualifiers. Robbie Keane grabs a goal in the last minute and the Waterford boys are heartened with the spirit the Irish team has shown. They only seem to play to their full potential when they go behind. A familiar trait.

'We're the very same,' Ó Líonáin agrees. 'We play better away from home and against good teams. For some reason we tend to sink a little when we play teams around the same level as ourselves. But sure maybe that's a good thing. We have the best two teams still to play.'

Mick O'Loughlin concurs: 'If we don't beat either Antrim or Sligo we have no business going up to Division 3 anyway. We have to be honest with ourselves too. But the only thing I want is that we go out fighting. I don't want to look back on the campaign and have London stand out as the reason we didn't make it up.

'I'll tell you one thing, though,' he adds, 'the preparation for the Sligo game will be spot-on. I'm going home now to write the itinerary myself.

If we have to spoonfeed the players that day we'll do it. Nothing will be left to chance, not the journey, the meal, the hydration. We have to make this work. I can guarantee we'll do all we can.'

The camp can almost see the end of their journey to escape the basement of Gaelic football. They have been here before, close to promotion, and they remain wary. The last leg is bound to have a few twists and turns yet.

Down here, no two roads are ever the same.

Chapter 11
Doing the Dual (Gary Hurney's Story)

Choosing the Hurley

I gave 11 years playing football for the county. I just felt it was time to give the hurling a real shot.

A lot of people out there probably feel I should have stayed with Jackson and the lads. Folk around here aren't slow to offer an opinion and plenty would think I'm not good enough to make the Waterford hurling team. But that doesn't bother me in the slightest. I'd be confident in my own ability and I'm positive.

I work hard, try to get a few scores from play, tear into tackles and do my best.

Football is my bread and butter but a decent run of hurling matches is all anyone needs. I've got that in 2009 and my touch has improved no end. I'm settling in and now the challenge is to show people that I'm not just a big lad who can win a ball in the air.

The criticism? Look, some people would be down on you straight away. They can't help it. The bottom line was that it was time to try something new.

Playing football, I've seen more bad times than most. Those dark oul days sap the life out of you but I don't tend to dwell too much on the past – the beatings and hammerings; they're all done and dusted. Consigned to history.

I want to win an All-Ireland medal with Waterford and, let's be honest, hurling is my only shot at realising that ambition.

There was no real way I could juggle both codes, although I would if I could. I'm still only 28 but I have over a decade of senior intercounty mileage clocked up and it doesn't be long affecting the engine power.

Having to choose between both wrecked my head for a while and it didn't help when people were telling me I should be doing this and that. Same with Shane Walsh.

Everyone was trying to tell us what to do. We did what we felt was right.

I actually began the season playing the first round of the McGrath Cup with the footballers. We beat Tralee IT that day but I was a bit distracted. Yeah, I did okay, got a goal and a couple of points, but I wasn't totally tuned in with the hurling calling.

There was talk around the county that Davy Fitzgerald had handed me an ultimatum – hurling or nothing – but it was entirely my decision to go with him. I wasn't forced or bullied into making it. The rest of the lads on the football team understood what I was at – some of them were in the same situation themselves in the past and they would have done the same thing.

With the hurlers you get the chance of playing in front of 20,000 and 30,000 people on most championship days and 82,000 if we reach an All-Ireland final. That's all new to me – I'm used to playing in front of 20 or 30. But you know what? It doesn't matter a hoot. I never trained to play in front of a crowd. There was an attendance of 5,000 down for our first match in the league against Tipp – but so what? You wouldn't be getting carried away with it.

Crowds are one thing, but it's only now that I can see the differences between the hurling and football camps. For a start, we have different types of fitness.

Then there's the mindset. In hurling, you might lose a game by just a point and the lads would be absolutely devastated – there would almost have to be a full-blown investigation into why that happened. Whereas, until recently, we could lose a football match by 20 or 30 points and still take some positives out of the result.

I'm deadly serious. I remember one day coming off the field after being hammered by Meath or someone and yet all we spoke about in the dressing room was how well Stephen Cunningham or one of the boys had played.

The footballers work just as hard as the hurlers, but obviously the hurlers have more strength in depth and more resources. Everything is on a plate for you. You don't need to ask. Things come a little easier for the hurlers and that's because we go looking to win each game we play.

The Football Omens

With the football we're getting there too. There were tough times in days gone by but it's been improving lately. We've had a bit of craic too, which kept the thing going.

The lads often tell the story about a time we travelled up north, a right slow crawl up the country to play Derry three or four years ago. On the way, Tom Condon put on the DVD of the famous Al Pacino 'inch by inch' speech from the movie *Any Given Sunday*. It's inspirational stuff and most of the top teams have used it at some stage to stoke them up before games. Tom and the boys decided it was our turn and they threw it on as the bus approached Celtic Park. By all accounts you could hear a pin drop – the lads were enthralled – but we lost the game by about 23 points.

I don't think the boys watched that film clip again.

Still, the mental attitude is changing. We have to cope with the huge number of lads who play club hurling and then there's plenty of players who don't believe they're as good as they actually are because we're used to being thrashed week in, week out.

137

I still remember my senior debut, for instance. It really couldn't have gone worse; we played Cork in the 1999 championship and they hockeyed us, 4-24 to 1-3.

But I also played on an U-21 team that beat Kerry in Killarney at the start of the decade and that was some result for us. It made up for all the shite. Wayne Hennessy, Ger Power, Mick Ahearne were on that team too and our confidence grew from there.

That result gave us some hope. It got people thinking about Waterford football – which really was a first.

It opened a door for me too. I had a shot at another life in 2000 when I was asked to attend an Australian Rules training camp at Dublin City University. There were a lot of players present for the trial, but one by one they dropped off as the coaches slashed them from the list. Right at the very end I found myself hanging in with two others, Joe Bergin from Galway and Tadhg Kennelly from Kerry. Only one could get the nod. Tadhg was that man and what a career he went on to have.

Sometimes I wonder what it would have been like over there but sure there would have been no guarantees. Tadhg's success was one in a million. You'd be too busy with the GAA to dwell on it too long or hard anyway. I was disappointed for a while but there were so many games to play back here, I wasn't long shaking it off.

Johnny Come Lately

Hurling and football have been my life since I was a kid. That's why I have no qualms about coming back in for the Sligo game. The lads have injuries and they need Shane and me. We're as fit as ever and we've been through more bad years than most of the boys, so I want to put all that right.

I know a few of the boys on the fringes of the team or lads on the bench will be pissed off to lose their chance of playing. They'll see us come in on a parachute. But it's not as if I'm a Johnny-come-lately – I'm one of them.

I've kept tabs on their results every week and was bloody horrified to hear about London. Their heads clearly weren't right for that one, but when they got back on track I knew they could make a real push for promotion.

Barring the top six or seven teams in the land, we're as good as any of the rest. People will laugh at that but I have no doubt – if we had a full team out and if there wasn't a problem with dual players we'd take on anyone.

Look at the lads we should have with us; the two Prendergasts, Séamus and Declan, are as good footballers as hurlers. Michael 'Brick' Walsh is possibly the best footballer in the county and Shane is class. You can throw my brothers, John and Patrick, into the mix as well.

But in Waterford hurling takes precedence. When you're called, you have to give it a shot – that's just the way it is. I'd love to see football getting equal treatment, and there's one thing that really bugs me – once the national league ends, the hurlers will get five weeks to prepare for their championship opener against Limerick. They'll have time to get things right and make the final tweaks. But when the Antrim game is out of the way and the curtain closes on the football league, the lads will be taken aside and asked to play senior club hurling for three weeks. And when that period ends, they'll have to play senior club football for the next two weeks. Then we play Cork in the Munster senior football championship.

That's a five-week break for the hurlers and a six-day gap for the footballers. How are you supposed to manage a team in those circumstances?

Somehow, Jackson holds the whole thing together. Lads play for him because of the man he is. There aren't too many people in the world like him.

I remember playing a league match up north somewhere a few years back and with 20 minutes to throw-in no one had seen sight nor sound of him. Eventually, they tracked him down via the mobile phone. He is big into Irish history and was visiting someone's grave a few miles up the road – someone who had been involved in the Troubles. Only Jackson.

He's been fair decent to me over the years and helped me get on the

Munster interprovincial football team. Sure he was always promoting me in public. He understands why I went with the hurlers – although he probably thought I'd be back as quick as I went.

I don't blame him either. If my senior hurling debut was an indicator I'd already be retired. It was as bad as my football debut.

Justin McCarthy called me up against Clare in 2008's championship and I must have been some kind of hoodoo because they pulverised us and I lost my place. Then Justin left, Davy took over and, in fairness, I've played a part in every game so far this season.

They played me at centre- and wing-forward early on, probably because I'm six-foot-three, but full-forward is where I play for my club, Abbeyside. And I'm at full-forward now, where I prefer to be.

Davy has confidence in me; he took me aside and showed me how to improve. It's the All-Ireland or nothing for him. Training has been dog-tough – non-stop stamina sessions first and then mostly ball work. But it won't make me any fitter when I go back playing football – it's like starting from scratch again. Hurling is all about speed and touch, football is tracking back, making support runs – you really can't compare them.

But I'll combine both for as long as the legs keep going. I started my career with the footballers and I'll probably end it with them too.

Chapter 12
The Promotion Dream

The Long Road to Sligo

11 April, Easter Saturday, Roosky, Roscommon

Forget London! The boys have clawed their way back into contention.

A win tomorrow and they'll most likely be promoted at the expense of their opponents.

Sligo – under their new manager, Kevin Walsh, a two-times All-Ireland medal winner with Galway – started the season like the biggest kids in the schoolyard. They may not have bragged about their prowess but they made Division 4 look too small for them. For a while they seemed invincible.

Lately, though, they've started to stutter. Defeat to Antrim last time out has left them just one point ahead of Waterford. And with the Ulstermen as good as promoted, this game will be a straight shootout between Walsh and Kiely to see who marches up to the lofty heights of Division 3.

Waterford would be ahead of Sligo were it not for the London fiasco. But they've bounced back impressively since then; they're still chasing the dream.

Tonight they rest up at the Shannon Key West Hotel in Roosky. Having left Dungarvan by bus at 3.30 p.m. and arrived here at 8.30 p.m., they're weary and a little cranky. It's been a long, coast-to-coast trek, made longer by the several pitstops to allow Jackson top up on nicotine.

At least their ravenous hunger has been fed – a chicken-salad supper promptly served up. Lessons have been learned, it seems.

As soon as they've been fed and watered, Jackson calls a team meeting and announces the starting 15. As expected, Gary Hurney and Shane Walsh are included.

They have a clearly defined job to do – grab scores – in what has lately been the most problematic sector of the field.

One by one, the manager goes through the starters and then turns to the panellists.

Knowing three or four of them are less than thrilled that Hurney and Walsh have gone straight into the side, he thanks each of the squad by name for commitment to the cause since the start of the season. He also reiterates that the prodigal sons are back with a mission – to get the team promoted.

'The two boys have seen as many bad years with Waterford football as anyone else in this room, myself included,' Jackson says. 'And now, just as we have a chance to have the best day in our history, they deserve a chance to play with us again. We need them, lads.'

It's clear the manager feels like a child on Christmas morning – this is as close to a perfect deck in terms of strength and quality as he'll ever have – and his words take the sulphur out of the atmosphere; the man has the happy knack of defusing the most explosive situations.

'Ger Power,' he shouts across the room. 'Would you mind telling me what was it like to be out injured, looking on at the lads for the past 12 months?'

He catches Power on the hop. The quiet man from Stradbally didn't expect he'd be called on to testify.

'Pure hell, really,' he responds. 'I was dying to get back. I could see the progress we were making and I wanted to return as quickly as possible. But it's great to be back with ye now – though I'm still only finding my feet.

But I'm getting there.'

Jackson turns to young Cillian O'Keeffe, probably the lightest player on the panel, not much more than five-foot-nine, but brave, highly mobile and blessed with an engine that runs and runs. His role has been mainly that of the impact sub, but he has impressed with his boundless enthusiasm and ability to find openings where none exist. Now he has the floor.

'Ah well, you just want to be on from the start,' he says, clearly also taken aback at being given centre stage.

'You train hard all year and you want to get a game but the competition is strong – you have to take your chance when it comes. I want to make the starting team and I'm ready to do a job if needed tomorrow. I don't train to be a sub but at the same time I'll do anything that's asked of me.'

With that, Jackson switches to analytical mode and goes through the Sligo team with forensic thoroughness.

'They have two good inside men, David Kelly and Adrian Marren, and they play Alan Costello as a playmaker across their midfield, but Eamonn O'Hara isn't fully fit and Mark Brehony isn't there either.'

And so he goes on, pointing up individual strengths and weaknesses as well as likely flaws in the collective, before putting things in a nutshell: 'They started the year like world beaters but now they're seeing what Division 4 is all about. They're there to be beaten. I could talk all day but I don't believe in psychology and all that shite. It's up to ye now, lads.'

With that, they retire to another room but it's not yet lights out. Jackson has one of his infamous table quizzes prepared, part of the ritual whenever they lodge together overnight. Very few people can match Jackson's *grá* for, or mastery of, history and general knowledge, and the questions he sets are of Mastermind standard. But the players love them and enter willingly into the fun, and on this night, after a comprehensive trawl through Irish and world history, the team made up of Tom Wall, Dave Kenneally and Ger Power emerges with bragging rights.

Contented and tired, the players head for their rooms and a hugely important night's sleep. Big game tomorrow. In fact a massive game. A game almost too big to bear thinking about. But sure isn't this what it's all about.

They've come a long way from Jackson's early training sessions – especially those ones where they struggled to get five players togged out.

* * *

12 April, Markiewicz Park, Sligo Town, County Sligo. NFL Round 6

Easter Sunday in Sligo. A bright afternoon and the air almost motionless under a warm sun.

After a breakfast of fruit, cereal, eggs and juice the lads are buzzing with energy. The vibes are good and confidence is high. Last evening's team talk and quiz have lifted spirits. They feel well prepared and ready for battle.

Throw-in is at 1p.m. They leave the hotel at 11.30 a.m. and travel the hour or so to the ground.

They have just arrived when Kevin Walsh, a gentle bear of a man, spots Jackson and is straight over with his hand out. Walsh was one of the best midfielders of the past decade and still cuts an impressive figure. After a spot of banter punctuated by hearty chuckles he heads away to attend to his troops. Jackson goes the other way. Both fighters into their corners, awaiting the bell.

Soon the Sligomen are out on the field, and the first impression among the Waterford guys is positive – these particular All Blacks are lacking in height and heft; some of them look callow.

Last out, however, is Eamonn O'Hara, not listed in the match programme but on his way back from a groin injury. You can tell from his movement he's not fully fit, but he's some player to have in reserve. This is the man who in 2007 shot the goal of the year to win the Connacht championship; on his day he's capable of just about anything on the football field.

Inside in their dressing room, the visitors, clad in white and blue, with minds focused, legs rubbed and sinews stretched, are going through their psychological fine-tuning.

The bellowing begins.

'Win today and we're on the way up,' Jackson roars. 'Shane Briggs, you're man-marking David Kelly – stick to him like fucking glue. Liam Lawlor, drop back into the usual role. Give them something to think about from the start.

'Lads, we have the talking done. A couple of years ago these guys won the Connacht title. They think they only have to go out there to win the game and go up a division.

But I know ye're as good as them – a fair whack of their players wouldn't make our team. I genuinely believe that.

'We're not going to get too psyched up – just go out there and play to the system. Gary and Shane are up in attack now, so work the ball to midfield like we always do and then go long to the two boys. We have options now, lads. Let's make the most of them! This is the best team ever fielded in the history of Waterford football. We deserve this!'

With a thunderous roar they sprint onto the field, down to the far end, and go into a 20-minute warm-up. At the other end, Sligo are busy too and their hits are noticeably ferocious. No fear, it seems, of them 'doing a Cavan' and underestimating Jackson's army.

The action gets underway. The stakes are high and the atmosphere is charged. Waterford get a dream start. Seán O'Hare gathers the ball, goes on a mazy run past four black jerseys, looks up and lets fly from 30 yards. The ball sails over the bar.

Pure class.

And then we get an explanation of all the hype about Hurney. He kicks a sublime point with his left boot from near the sideline.

Walsh, the other dual in the crown, is only half Hurney's size but is fielding like a salmon among mayfly. He also scores early on. And when Liam Ó Líonáin ghosts through the Sligo defence before pointing, it seems the home side are there for the taking.

145

The Sligo fans are stunned. The two Waterford supporters present – Brian Wall's parents, to be specific – greet each score with lusty applause.

After 23 minutes it's 0-6 to 0-2. Then the black sea parts again and Paul Ogle, who has raced upfield from wing-back, finds himself with the ball and in acres of space.

There are two options – pass inside to Hurney and the goal is on or pop it over himself. He gets caught in two minds and picks the ball off the floor before shooting a point, which is disallowed.

This is the spur for Sligo to react. They replace their centre-back Brendan Phillips and wing-back Michael McNamara and begin to steady the ship. By the end of the half they have cut the deficit to three points.

Promotion Pitstop

In the dressing room, Paul McLoughlin is first to his feet.

'You're playing fantastic stuff,' he says. 'Just take your chances as they come and be a bit surer of yourselves when you're attacking. Get the ball and distribute it quicker.

'Fair play to ye for finding Gary and Shane quickly, but don't give them Hail Mary balls all the time either – give them something to work with. But, lads, ye're doing exactly what's being asked of ye. I'm delighted. We're well on top.'

Hurney speaks up.

'Lads, is there one player on their team that we would take the way we are playing? No, there's not. We're by far the better side – they don't know what's hit them.'

Now it's Jackson's turn.

'What did I tell ye, lads?' he yelps. 'We're better than them. We have seven players who played for Munster on our team and we're a better side.'

There's a pregnant pause. Whenever Jackson speaks, he is liable to produce a wild card, and you sense one coming now. And this time he really plays a joker. Turning from his players he addresses your embedded correspondent – the lad in the corner sipping tea, taking mental notes and generally trying to look invisible.

'Well, Damian, what do you think?'

To say that the silence is stunned would be only the half of it.

Suddenly it hits home. Jesus Christ, he's talking to me.

'Ah, erm, umm,' I splutter as the players fix me with expectant or bemused stares.

Jackson coaxes.

'Hey, c'mon, Damian – you've seen a thousand games over the past ten years. What do you think? Are our lads as good as anyone or what?'

'They are,' I stutter, seriously embarrassed, blood rushing to my face.

Inspirational stuff, Lawlor. They'll be running out the door with fire in their hearts after that speech. William Wallace isn't a patch on you.

He caught me with a curve ball. Since the start of this adventure, the players have welcomed me warmly, but in the dressing room I've kept a low profile. In fact I've treated the dressing room like a flight with Ryanair – grab the first available seat and keep the mouth shut and the head bowed. It was all working just fine till now.

The subs chuckle heartily at my discomfort. But I'm ready to kick myself. It's not too often I'm caught for words. And secretly my inner coach wanted to leap up and roar at them to believe in themselves. I wanted to tell Liam Lawlor he was the best player on the field and would make any team in the land playing that quarter-back role of his.

I wanted to grab Ó Líonáin, shake him well and remind him he can be one of the most explosive forwards in the game.

I really wanted to lay my cards on the table and tell the lads how fond I had grown of them, to tell them to do it for Jackson, the man who had brought them all together.

But I am a journalist. Among players. Shut up. They don't want to hear my views.

Why would they?

Thankfully, Shane Briggs comes to my rescue and breaks the silence.

'Fuck it, lads, it's our big chance. Never mind the scoreboard, play the way we have been and we get on the bus in an hour's time with two points in the bag. A few early scores and these lads are buried. We're all around long enough now, we've had all the disappointment over the years – let's change that.'

The team huddle around and someone lets a shout: 'One goal will finish this lot!'

That remark is uttered in the heat of the moment and with the best of intentions. But it will soon return to haunt them.

When they go back out, Sligo take them apart like a butcher filleting a joint of meat. Eddie Rockett ships an early injury and cannot sprint. Mick Ahearne has struggled with illness in the previous weeks and fades disastrously in midfield. But worst of all, Waterford try to go for goal after goal instead of tipping the ball over the bar.

Meanwhile, Sligo post six points without reply and run the visiting half-backs ragged.

With 15 minutes to go they lead by four points.

What a turnaround! How could it all fall apart so quickly?

That old chestnut again. When you're down and you don't know anything else, it's hard to escape the rut for fear of what the light will do to you.

And then, suddenly, a fresh chink of hope. A high ball is boomed across the square to Shane Walsh, who makes a miraculous catch. Bang and goal! The Waterford bench erupts in delight. The air gets punched. Game on again.

Back come Sligo with points from Marren and Shane Stenson and then, with time running out, ultimate agony for Waterford. Hurney has long since moved out to midfield to paper over the cracks. He feeds the attack with a gorgeous ball. Ó Líonáin punches the ball and it looks to be unstoppable. But Philip Greene, the Sligo keeper, dives full-length to his right to pull off

148

the save of the century.

It clinches the game; Sligo hang on to win 0-16 to 1-11.

Soon incredible news filters through from Aughrim – Carlow have beaten Wicklow, the other late contenders in the divison. Promotion is officially Sligo's. Same old story for Waterford.

They came so close but they're back in that desolate and drearily familiar place. A glance across the field reveals mass devastation, physical exhaustion, mental anguish.

They've expended so much in hope and expectation that they cannot summon words.

Down at the other end, Sligo are simply too weary to celebrate. They've been in a shootout and know they have dodged the bullet.

'We sat down at the start of the year and targeted three teams that were going to give us serious trouble,' says Eamonn O'Hara, who came off the bench when they were struggling to stay afloat.

'Those teams were Antrim, Waterford and Wicklow and we were proved right. I've played against Waterford twice in the past few years; they beat us once and we were lucky they didn't beat us the second time. So I'm not one bit surprised with the way they played here.

'We didn't take them lightly. We are in Division 4 for a reason, so we have no right to be going around the place with fucking arrogance or anything like that. We respected Waterford and do you know why? Because they came here today to play football – there was no negativity or any of that shit. They tore into us and we tore into them.

'Wide open. Fucking great match.'

And yet his words are of little or no comfort.

The visitors' team room is like a morgue. Briggs hold his head in his hands for 20 minutes without budging. The O'Gormans are ashen-faced, Ó Líonáin looks like he's in physical agony. Tom Wall, a man who has let in only one goal all year, is destroyed. No one speaks except for Hurney, who tries to raise spirits.

'Lads, I've been with Waterford football for 10 years and I've never played on a team that showed the skill and intensity we showed out there – never. I know you won't look on it now but there are huge positives to be taken from this game. It was a great contest. Maybe the better team won but to play to that level was a wonderful thing. It will stand to us, lads. No doubt about it.'

His words provide little solace but he's not far wrong. Some of the football today was sensational. Due credit to Lawlor, the class act on the field. He got on the ball 34 times and didn't surrender it once; there was no one out there to touch him. He could grace any team in the land and sprinkle some quality.

But stillness again, save for the drip-drip splashing off the shower-room tiles. The players shuffle around the dressing room, towel themselves down and make their way back on board the team bus. They stop off at Roosky for dinner. Silence all around.

'That game was our All-Ireland final,' Jackson reflects ruefully. 'It's fair disappointing, I'll tell you that.'

They came to Sligo and hoped to leave with a bang. As the bus eases out onto the Dublin road, though, there's barely a whimper to be heard.

Bitter disappointment. The staple diet for a Waterford footballer.

Changes for Antrim

18 April, Fraher Field, Dungarvan, County Waterford. NFL Round 7

It all means that this game is about as meaningful as a sure-thing promise from a serial flirt. Antrim are already assured of a route to Division 3 and there can be no harvest of gold for Waterford.

So Jackson rests several of his leading names and gives the support cast a chance. And would you believe it, his second string are absolutely skinning the Ultermen. With the wind gusting at their backs they lead by four points.

After about 20 minutes the Northerners start making changes but to little avail. For one 38-minute spell Liam Bradley's team fail to score from play. It's baffling. Not only are this lot no better than a second-string Waterford, they look a hell of a lot worse.

Hurney and Walsh have gone back hurling with Davy Fitzgerald. Mick Ahearne is out with a mystery illness, Thomas O'Gorman has headed for New Zealand for two weeks. Eddie Rockett and Stephen Cunningham are injured.

To further stretch Waterford resources, their midfield general Seán O'Hare incurs the ref's disapproval and sees yellow. He's been the undoubted man of the match, and on the day GAA Congress votes to scrap the experimental rules, it seems ridiculous that he should have to leave the field for a hefty shoulder charge.

Meanwhile, Ó Líonáin is skinning the Antrim men, stepping around them like a tap dancer on amphetamines. He's managed 6-15 from play in this year's league, a sensational tally – no other player has managed six goals from play in any of the four divisions.

When O'Hare leaves the field, however, the unit starts to lose cohesion. By now they're mostly bit players, and while the likes of Cillian O'Keeffe and Tony Grey have made huge contributions, others struggle to keep Antrim at bay. They start fouling, and Antrim's Paddy Cunningham – he of the sweet left boot – points five or six frees in rapid succession.

Antrim win 0-13 to 0-8. They will play Sligo in the league final the following weekend while all Waterford can do is turn their attention to Cork and the championship.

Actually they can't. In any other county, the entire focus would now be on the summer but here the footballers go back to their clubs to play senior and junior hurling championship games for the next two weekends. That's some preparation for the Cork game: two weeks of hurling with their clubs.

'There's nothing I can do about it,' Jackson sighs. 'Sure I don't want the lads going away getting injured but I can't rock the boat either. We have to keep our heads down as much as possible in this county to get any bit of goodwill. It took an awful lot to get Gary and Shane back for the last match, so I can't stop the lads hurling.

'Most of them are real good hurlers anyway. Brian Wall, Wayne Hennessy, Liam Lawlor, Stephen Cunningham, Eddie Rockett – they've all hurled senior for the county. Seán O'Hare, the O'Gormans, Liam Ó Líonáin, Shane Briggs – they're all decent hurlers and play senior for their clubs. I think 12 of my starting 15 against Sligo play senior hurling at home.'

He'll have to wave goodbye to them all for a fortnight and then just two weeks before the Cork match he'll get them back again. Any or all of them could pick up serious knocks but Kiely sees no advantage in bitching.

'There's really nothing I can do,' he shrugs. 'The lads owe a duty to their clubs.'

But for all the commendable stoicism, you can see the frustration etched on his face.

Another season has come and gone without promotion and it hurts like hell. It would be one thing if the team weren't good enough to make the step up but they are. They just lack consistency and a killer instinct. You could say they are too nice to their opponents. They had Wicklow, London, Sligo and Antrim on the rack and yet they let each of them slip their chains. That's what cost them.

'I prefer to look back on the positives first,' Jackson muses. 'Take small Tom Wall. That's 13 games he's played for me in the past two years and he's only conceded one goal. That's incredible. We're talking 12 league games, eight this year and four last year. The only goal he let in was in the championship match with Clare last season. I mean, 12 clean sheets out of 13 and not a word in the press about the lad.

'And there's Ó Líonáin. Christ Almighty. And Liam Lawlor – I would say he is one of the best players in the division. And the O'Gormans are even better than they were last season. Seán O'Hare is a massive plus –

he's the best midfielder in the division at the moment. I would also consider it a huge plus that we got two hurling lads to play with us against Sligo. Please God, they'll be with us for the Cork game too. And Patrick Hurney has been dropped from the hurling squad so he'll be back.'

And the negatives?

'There are a few, no point in saying otherwise. The London game still amazes me.

'How we failed to put the ball over the bar I don't know. We came out on top in the Carlow game but our display was cruel – we should have won it handy. I was also disappointed with the way we handled Leitrim. We struggled with the scoring again. Sligo and Wicklow. We should have won both – we certainly could've won both.

'I genuinely think that had we been at full strength we could have been the best team in the division. Sure the Antrim game was a joke – we made seven changes from the week before.

'Yeah, those are regrets, I suppose. When I see Tipperary promoted as champions to Division 2 that really drives it home for me. I'm thrilled for them but sure there was never more than a point or two between us for the past few years.'

Mick O'Loughlin, the Tipp native, is equally delighted for his own county but would probably have swapped it all to see Waterford make the breakthrough. He too is philosophical as he reflects on the campaign.

'Drawing with Wicklow seemed to put us on the right path but we could have even snatched a win. Kilkenny again proved we were going in the right direction. We only beat them by seven points last year. For me, our display against Clare was our performance of the league. We scored 15 points in Ennis and took control of the second half. We looked a mature side and remained undefeated. But what a nightmare in London – it cost us promotion.

'On the management side, we have to hold our hands up and say that our planning for London should have been more precise and detailed. I still believe we should have had a team meeting on the morning of the game.

'Liam Lawlor's absence proved very significant. His stats on possession in the other games showed he was the vital cog in our gameplan, our link man. His decision not to travel was very costly for us. We also came up against a referee who gave a shocking display in not implementing the new rules. All the linesmen and umpires were from London and were of no assistance to him – there were third-man tackles all over the place.

'We all felt responsible for the defeat and our wins against Leitrim and Carlow proved there was determination to put things right. Other teams would have folded but not our crew.

'Overall, it's very disappointing for two years in a row to miss out on promotion by losing very winnable games. But there was a huge effort put in by everyone. After coming so far over the five years, to be denied promotion again is hard to take. This bunch deserve to be promoted.'

There's little time to sit back and mope, though. If they do that, Cork will wipe the field with them in the Munster championship and that sickening feeling will persist.

Jackson is already looking ahead, knowing that wallowing in their league failures will surely sink their championship hopes.

'The truth is that we have seven or eight very high-quality players, and hopefully none of them will get injured for Cork,' he says. 'We'll get a few more in to strengthen the panel but I'll be cutting the squad to 24. There's no point in carrying lads. Even though a few showed up well early in the year, they've not all made much progress.

'They're all nice young lads, from decent families, and letting them go won't be the nicest part of my job, but I won't be writing letters or sending texts. No, I'll meet them one by one and explain to them why they're being let go.'

Straight up, that's the only way Kiely does business.

Clubs v County

With most of the team now club-tied, the players are told there will be just four training sessions – and two get-togethers, just to keep the continuity going – between now and the Cork match. It's a disaster. What hope have they?

'A joke,' agrees Paul McLoughlin. 'It's cruel that we're even in this situation – all our focus should be on the championship but this is the way it is down here. What can you do? I'll tell you what you can do – allow your top players to play football if they want; give the football team a proper chance to prepare for the championship. Our biggest hope over the next few weeks is that half of our team won't get injured. Cork will be laughing at us.

'I have no problem with the individual members of the county board – they seem like solid enough guys. But what's put before us is an absolute and utter disgrace. Our boys have put in a great effort in the league. They've come up short but now they'll come back to us knackered and hurt after two weeks of club hurling. We won't get a chance to train them properly. We'll probably have to fucking rest them. All this before a championship match against the third-best team in Ireland? A joke.'

Nonetheless, the backroom team have to keep a brave face. If they lose faith the players will pick up on it and be tempted to jack it in.

Meanwhile, management have been looking all over the county for talent. There's a spot of housekeeping needed. Five players are dropped from the squad and another four are asked to continue training but will most likely be used by the county juniors on match day. The seniors and juniors play Cork on the same day in Fraher Field.

The five to go include Seán Fleming, who managed 0-7 in seven league games, not bad by the rest of the team's standards, but not enough to save him from the chop.

Seán Dempsey, an All-Ireland junior winner, saw very little action throughout the spring and also loses out. John Hayden, who, like Dempsey, was based in Dublin and trained with John O'Mahony's Mayo camp, is another to miss the cut. Martin Whelan was only drafted into the league squad late on and also gets the bad news.

Stephen Prendergast, Michael O'Gorman, Dermot Casey and Brian Phelan are retained on the training panel but will have to be ready to line out with the juniors. Gary and Patrick Hurney, Shane Walsh and the fit-again Justin Walsh are potential additions. Two 18-year-olds, Brian O'Halloran and Shane Aherne, have caught the selectors' eye over the past few weeks. Despite their youth they are invited to train with the team.

'At this stage they should be brought in, if only to give the lads something to think about,' McLoughlin says. 'We have to build for the future anyway, whether we are here or not next year. We're better having a base of young lads rather than carrying guys in their late 20s who will not figure no matter how stuck we are.

'Everyone will have us written off for the Cork game, and while we'll be all out to cause a huge shock the bottom line is we also have to be ready for the qualifiers. And I firmly believe there are about 10 teams out there that we could beat in the qualifiers – if we get a bit of luck with the draw.

'I think with a bit of luck we could get a couple of games out of the summer – even if our lads are going to be hunted down by their clubs.

'That's one thing I would look for next season, whether or not we are still around. No one in his right mind should take the job as Waterford football manager until he has it on paper from the county board that he will get four weeks to prepare the team for a championship match and not be stuck with this nonsense of seeing players taken away for domestic hurling fixtures.

'What are the chances of that happening? I don't know.'

Slim and none at the moment.

Chapter 13
Inside the Team

The O'Gormans' Grief
---·---

24 April, Blanchardstown, Dublin

Dusk falls over Blanchardstown as Thomas O'Gorman unwinds in his digs. He pauses for breath, tired after the working day. Battling rush-hour traffic is something he will never get used to but for the time being it's his lot.

He works as a construction planner and has been in Dublin over a year now. Not a day goes by that he doesn't contemplate getting work closer to home, but in the current slump he's just glad of what he has – no matter where it is.

O'Gorman is one of a family of eight children. They come from Glasha, a lovely village nestled between the Knockmealdown and Comeragh mountains. All around lies terrain made for hillwalking. It's idyllic, blissfully peaceful, a world removed from the concrete suburban sprawl of Dublin 15.

'Some day soon I'll get back down around home,' he says softly. 'It would be handy for training, above anything else.'

For Thomas and his twin, Maurice, this is a fourth season with the county team. Michael, their younger brother, joined them in January 2009. They play football for The Nire and hurl for Fourmilewater, and at weekends they link up with Jackson's Army.

Their days are varied to say the least. Whereas the likes of The Nire and Stradbally are well capable of making an impression countrywide, the county footballers are a more fragile species. Slowly though, thanks to the likes of the magnificent O'Gormans, they are gaining strength.

Sportswise, Thomas has a generous sheaf of options; scarcely a weekend goes by all year when he doesn't have a game to play. Last weekend, he lined out at corner-forward for Fourmilewater against Ballyduff Upper in the Waterford senior hurling championship. He managed a goal and a point and they were set for a fine win until a late smash-and-grab gave Ballyduff victory by a point.

Disappointment haunted him afterwards but there was little time for wallowing – he had to turn his thoughts to Mount Sion and the second round next weekend.

'I would find it hard to choose between hurling and football,' he says. 'I'll hurl away for my club but the football is everything to me as well. So I just take it week by week, focus on whatever game is coming up. Sure the brothers are like that as well.'

GAA has played a massive part in his life. His father, John, started the ball rolling by taking him to club games as a grasshoppper. He grew up watching The Nire and Fourmilewater, and so playing for them seemed the logical corollary. Over the years he has racked up appearances for club, college, county and Munster. Both codes come easy to him and Maurice. The O'Gormans don't do flustered.

Being part of so many teams has stood to them of late. The past 12 months have been cruel on the family. Last July they lost their mother, Kathleen, and eight months later their dad passed away after a short illness. Coping with such a double loss is almost unimaginable but it's become a grim reality for Thomas and the rest of the clan. Thank God there is support in numbers – as well as Thomas there are four boys and three girls in the family – and strength in unity.

John died just hours after the NFL game against Clare. In the dressing room Jackson praised the brothers for their contribution to the team, and that game was dedicated to them. Just a week later, the three of them were back in the camp and they all played against London.

'It came as a bit of a shock to us the way it just happened,' Thomas says. 'It was hard to take. After the funeral Maurice, Michael and I spoke about what we would do about the football and during the week we just decided that we were better off going over playing with the lads rather than just sitting around at home thinking of it. Sure what good would that do?

'I'm not saying we were fully prepared going over to London – but it was better than just staying home doing nothing. It helped to take our minds off things. The lads on the team were great – a lot of them turned up at the funeral and paid their respects. So coming back and being part of the team again helps.

'I suppose after the year or so that we've had it's only then you fully realise how important the GAA is. You're playing with friends and people you admire and it's something to focus on.

'Jackson was very good to us. He rang us and arranged that the boys on the team turned up for a guard of honour. It meant a lot. The oul fella was a huge GAA man anyway – he would have wanted us getting back as soon as we could.'

And so they flew out to Ruislip with the rest of the panel, togged out and played in a disaster of a game. Truth be told, Thomas just wanted to get out of the Big Smoke and head straight back home after the match.

'Ah, sure you just wanted to be anywhere but London after losing,' he recalls. 'But eventually a few lads got together that night and we tried to put it behind us. The rest of that night is just a bit of a blur really.'

Deeply disappointed at how the league campaign petered out, he feels it's important the team now reassesses goals for the year, especially with the club hurling championships pilfering most of their players for the time being.

'Yeah, the local hurling has taken over now and it's not ideal. I would have been looking for a training camp for three weeks before we played Cork but there's no hope. They are flying at the moment and will come at us with all guns blazing. I still reckon, though, that if we have our full team we can get some respectability out of that. And even if we don't manage to beat them, the goal for the year has to be to win a qualifier game. That's hugely important. But we'll need a bit of luck with the draw. If we get that, I reckon there are definitely six or seven teams we would be well capable of beating.

'So while there's a danger that the season could disintegrate I don't think the lads will settle for that. Too much work has been put in. There were training sessions where lads were heaving at the start of the year and you don't just let that effort slide away. It has to count for something. We have to make it count.'

Fearless O'Keeffe

4 May, Clashmore, West Waterford

At the start of the year, with the Cork hurlers deep in strike mode, Cillian O'Keeffe received a circular email from Donal Óg Cusack, the Cork goalkeeper and Gaelic Players' Association chairman. The email was an effort to enlighten other intercounty players as to the issues at stake in the Rebels' strike. Essentially, Cusack was explaining Cork's plight and asking GPA members for support.

But there was little sign of solidarity in the email O'Keeffe fired back in reply.

'Hey, stop sending me this rubbish,' was the gist. 'Either go back and play with your county or retire.'

He reckons that put a full stop to the correspondence. He heard no more.

What you see with this lad is what you get. The squad has been away from camp for the bones of a week now but O'Keeffe is already itching to get back. And he doesn't hesitate to explain why.

'I understand the club hurling has to be allowed space on the calendar but we have a huge game against Cork coming up too. We should be in getting ready for that. I hate the waiting around.'

He admits that initially he welcomed the break.

'But I'm plain sick of it now,' he moans. 'I love going in and pushing myself hard. I love being fit and love the feeling you get after training when you've given everything. Even though we've only missed three or so sessions since the league ended I have enough of sitting around in the evenings now.'

A fresher at WIT, he studies the wonderfully titled 'Entertainment Systems'. Carlsberg don't do college courses but if they did this would surely be one of them.

'I have to admit it sounds amazing,' he laughs. 'It's actually a cross between music technology and games development but it's tough enough too. At least I have an interest in that field – I gave a couple of years studying computer science in UCC before that.'

At 23, O'Keeffe isn't your quintessential senior county footballer. He's no more than five-ten and is one of the lightest men in intercounty football. You wonder that he hasn't been blown out of it by now.

'It's the first thing people say when they see me playing,' he smiles. 'But sure I know I'm only a skinny little runt. Therefore I find other ways to be of use. Work-rate is my thing – I would cover ground from the moment the game starts to the second it ends.

'Although I'm at a huge disadvantage because I'm a skinny oul string, I can make up for it because I'm very fit. Which is just as well because no matter what I do I cannot fatten up. I've tried four protein shakes a day but not a hope of even putting on a pound. I'm still the same size as always, maybe even lighter.'

What he lacks in bulk he makes up for in bravery. He isn't afraid to get stuck in or throw his body in harm's way. The selectors like that quality and have used him in most games this season. They don't really have an out-and-out position for him; he just goes on and covers every blade of grass, providing the team with a link-man, a bit of pace and some extra defensive cover.

'I play at full-forward for Clashmore but it would be very frustrating playing there for the county because they usually look for a target man, and then we have the short-passing game, so you wouldn't be strong enough to win ball and it would be slow in coming into you too,' he explains.

'I know that I don't exactly have the prowess to be a big, powerful threat on the edge of the square so I just make up ground, look for the ball, lay it off and on I go again.'

He didn't pick that zest off a bush; it comes from a family with an impressive GAA lineage. Timmy, his father, is a former Waterford football goalkeeper and coach. He has just been appointed full-time county secretary and already it's clear he shoots from the hip, is organised and has a vision. His appointment has gone down well with the round-ball community.

While Timmy charts the way forward for Waterford GAA, his son continues to represent them on the field.

'I've played with Waterford at every grade from U-14,' he says. 'I think Stevie Prendergast and I are the two who've been together right from the start and I'm fierce proud of that. I would be dead serious about it – there's no point in just turning up for a jersey at the end of the year.'

Directing his thoughts to the weeks ahead, he says he will have plenty of motivation for the Cork game.

'A lot of people will feel the curtains will close on our season by June and maybe it will, but I think our biggest game will be in the qualifiers,' he muses. 'Realistically, we will have it all to do to beat Cork. I mean, they are absolutely flying and will push hard for an All-Ireland title.

'I would be the happiest man in Ireland to beat them – I spent two years with the UCC Sigerson Cup team and I know a lot of them. The Cork lads back themselves, always have done, and it would be nice to test them. But you would have to say we're more likely to get something out of the qualifiers provided we get a half-decent draw. At least it would really be in our own hands then.

'Maybe we shouldn't get too bogged down with the Cork game and should make sure we are peaking for the qualifiers. I know people won't agree with that – it's just my thoughts.'

With that he's back to the books, ready for the year's final exams. Driving out of Clashmore you can clearly see Drum Hills and the River Blackwater. The village is distinguished by its brightly painted houses. Signposts indicate a wealth of heritage sites; and there are adverts for fishing, watersports and golf. But as he tends to his studies, O'Keeffe has time for none of these. He just wants to get the swotting out of the way and get back to the football. As soon as possible.

Hayden – Hanging Out to Dry
—·—

10 May, Tramore, County Waterford

If O'Keeffe can't wait to get back to the training field, it's a different story entirely for John Hayden, the young defender from the east of the county, a section that's struggling to provide players for the football team.

2009 began brightly for him; he played all three games of the McGrath Cup but he can't seem to buy a slice of action since then. He spent the spring wrapped up in tracksuits.

Last week he got the call from Jackson asking him to go back and play with the juniors but the text messages from the senior squad have stopped beeping on his phone. He's an intelligent guy, has five years in college behind him and doesn't need an honours degree to tell him he's been dropped.

'John rang me and told me to get a few games in with the juniors but, yeah, when the texts stopped coming through I more or less knew where I was at,' he smiles ruefully.

Naturally enough he's disappointed. He joined the team for the Tommy Murphy campaign last year and put in a massive effort since January, training both at home and in Dublin, where he's been studying.

Twice a week, Hayden met with a group of more than 30 intercounty footballers. Most hailed from Mayo, but there were men from Wexford, Fermanagh and Cavan too; young men working in the metropolis, most of them more than 100 kilometres from home.

Training in Dublin keeps them focused and helps them climb out of bed and go to work the next morning properly stretched and hydrated, not crippled from a gruelling car journey home and not starved of sleep after travelling half the night.

The Garda Sports and Social Club in Westmanstown, near Lucan, is their second home. Each Tuesday night they work out under the tutelage of John O'Mahony, TD and Mayo manager.

Hayden and his Waterford teammate Seán Dempsey heard about the sessions and asked if they could tag along. Jason Ryan made some calls; a few of his Wexford lads are part of the group and he had the connections. And so since January, the two Waterford boys have been on board. They are hugely enthusiastic.

'It's absolutely ridiculous how good the set-up is,' Hayden says. 'You don't get a break at all during the 90 minutes. When you've finished speed or stamina drills you pop over to another coach for football work. And vice-versa. It's 100 miles per hour. There's no standing around – cones are laid out all over the field and it's whirlwind stuff. We would often do drills or play matches between ourselves and I took my fair share of roastings at the start but you soon cop on.'

At first they felt like tenant labourers invited to dine in the Big House. Most of the group were pushing for provincial honours or better. But, Hayden says, they were treated the same as everyone else; they were footballers trying to better themselves.

'No one ever looked down on Seán or I because of where we were from. When we first came we knew no one, but by the end of the season we were like a big family. There were about 38 regulars and you would look forward to it. It was almost like we were a team ourselves.

'But what I really couldn't believe was the way we were treated after training. In fairness, the Waterford board paid for Seán and me, which meant we could do the training, use the facilities and get the meals afterwards.'

Hayden was queueing for a bit of grub after the first session when he saw the menu. His jaw dropped – there were three courses

'I said to one of the lads: "Jesus, isn't this great?" He looked at me and asked what I was on about. I remarked how good the choice of food was. He said every team in Ireland got that after training. I said nothing, but he asked me again what I was on about. I just muttered something about a fellow mostly coming into our dressing room with a drum of food and us eating it on our laps off paper plates. Your man just shook his head. Couldn't believe it.'

Hayden has just graduated from UCD as a physio and plans to travel to New Zealand to work for two years, so being dropped from the Waterford set-up isn't the end of the world.

'Nah, it's not,' he agrees, 'whether I was team captain or last sub I was always off to New Zealand to work, but I suppose I would liked to have had more of a chance to make the team. I played throughout the McGrath Cup but they preferred Mark Prendergast to me in the league and fair enough, he's been there before.

'There were times during the season when I thought I might be in with a shout but all I got was five minutes against Antrim, near the end of a match – that meant nothing. That was hard to take. It was even harder when the likes of Gary and Shane came straight back into the team despite not training with us. The two lads are lovely blokes but it kind of sent out a wrong message to the rest of us. No point in saying otherwise.

'Still, I have nothing against anyone. John Kiely is one of the soundest men you'll meet, so genuine, and I really enjoyed my time with the lads and the backroom boys. We had some craic along the way.

'And you know what? I'll be able to apply for physio jobs with a bit more confidence now. Having a CV that shows you played intercounty football will definitely stand to you. Jobs are scarce here at the moment – hence the trip to New Zealand – so that will stand to me.'

Hayden didn't let the season merely peter out. He's been heavily involved with the Tramore footballers and they're motoring well in the club championship. He also manned the centre-back berth for the Waterford juniors against Cork, though that experience didn't exactly boost his self-belief.

'If you think the Waterford senior footballers are treated badly you'd want to see the juniors,' he smiles. 'We had two weeks to prepare for that game. We only had a short time together. In the dressing room someone tried to explain that we had to keep the costs down and training to a minimum.'

Still, he's the type of guy who will look back on the season and take the positives, not the negatives.

'Absolutely,' he says. 'I would look back at the London game and, as a physio, I think Liam Ó Líonáin was injured that day and shouldn't have been left on the field.

'Maybe bringing the two boys back from the hurling team could have been handled differently. They are two of the best footballers in the county but we needed to see them training with us. I probably stopped caring when all that happened but that's it. Those are just football issues that will arise in any team.

'I certainly couldn't hold anything against the rest of the lads. They brought me along and hopefully I improved. I'm young and, you never know, I could get back again. It's still a great achievement to have played senior intercounty football. I'll always have that.'

Aherne's Agony

13 May, Lattin, County Tipperary

The Waterford club hurling championship is in full flow, but Jackson has rustled up a team to play Clare in a football challenge. The sides meet at an agreed midway point: Lattin, a village of about 20 houses on the edge of the Tipp-Limerick border.

Like most tiny parishes in Ireland, Lattin has a splendid GAA club. This one is particularly neat; the pitch is pristine and surrounded by a lovely, compact stand that complements it nicely. It's also the home of Nicky English, the legendary Tipperary hurler and manager. Tonight, his clubmen have made their place available.

Not that either Waterford or Clare will have a full side. It turns out to be a completely meaningless affair. Waterford manage to produce two subs, and the body language of those on the field suggests this is the last place they want to be. They are in the middle of a hectic hurling schedule and, to be blunt, their legs are sapped of energy.

Patrick Hurney is back in harness, having been released by the hurlers, but despite training almost daily under Davy Fitz he looks nowhere near football-fit. It's going to take him some time to get up to speed.

While most of the team wish they were at home watching Man United virtually clinching the Premiership away to Wigan, it's heartening to see that some are making a real effort. Stephen Cunningham, back from a finger injury, is all action; Paul Ogle is up and down the field after every ball; Eddie Rockett manages a goal after a run from centre-back. Waterford lead for most of the 70 minutes but concede a late goal and lose. Not that they're worried.

It must be said that Clare are fitter than when the sides last met in the league. Are they better? No. It's just that Waterford this time are worse. For the record, Clare win 1-9 to 1-7 in what must be one of the worst intercounty games ever played.

Waterford gave the ball away an incredible 18 times in the first half. But Clare didn't know what to do with it, and woeful shooting prevented them winning by a basketball score. Even their free-taker David Tubridy, normally on target, was misfiring.

Late in the first half, Tom Wall trudges ashen-faced from his goalmouth to the sideline. Kiely walks over and throws a sympathetic arm around his keeper's shoulder.

'It must be fair bad if Tom is coming off,' the manager says. 'The man loves his football.'

It emerges that while playing for Bunmahon the night before, Wall had his helmet split by a flying hurley. He's dizzy, nauseated and stiff-necked. It's time for an X-ray.

As the pocket battleship disappears into the changing room, the giant figure of Glenn Kelly, the TG4 'Underdog', replaces him. Kelly will tog out for the Waterford juniors against Cork before benching as sub-keeper for the seniors after that game.

Stephen Enright, the usual reserve, has broken a leg playing hurling for Abbeyside and his season is as good as over. Kelly, a native of Dublin, has just transferred to Waterford and will get a good dollop of intercounty football over the next few weeks.

He fares well and can do nothing about the late goal as his adopted team lose a game they should have won – even in their dishevelled state. Still, as they dissect the 70 minutes, the backroom are philosophical.

'At least we got the lads back together and playing again,' Kiely says. 'It was beneficial from that point of view. The Cork game is only around the corner. We needed to see them once more.'

Another challenge, this time against London the following Saturday night at Walsh Park, is announced in the dressing room. Players immediately question the need to play 'that lot' again. It turns out the Exiles are in Ireland preparing for their championship opener against Galway and they want games. They played Wexford the week before and ran them to four points. Now they've taken advantage of the recession and arranged a cut-price weekend in Waterford – and Kiely has agreed to a rematch.

The hope is that the team will burn with motivation, strike up a nice score, exact sweet revenge for the league defeat and proceed to the Cork game with confidence high and swords sharpened.

But the opposite happens. Half the team are injured, and they have only one sub, Cillian O'Keeffe, who is picked at corner-back. When they get the ball they can't hold onto it. And when they do lose possession they're not all that interested in getting it back. No one plays well and London take the home side apart. In the end it's a hammering, 2-13 to 1-7. There are problems in every area of the pitch.

To say the bottom has fallen out of the whole season is to put it mildly.

Mick Ahearne has missed the challenge-circuit double bill. The Fermoy-based schoolteacher hasn't been himself these past eight weeks and tests have shown he's had a blood disorder since the Carlow game. He was hauled off at a crucial point during the Sligo game, a strange sight for anyone familiar with the scene this past decade. Normally, Ahearne is the one they look to when the going gets tough. So it was depressing to see him substituted with that game hanging in the balance.

Many of those present felt at the time it was simply the unofficial but inevitable changing of the midfield guard, that after a decade on top of his game Ahearne had no choice but to hand the baton to Seán O'Hare. It turns out, though, that he had no business being out on the paddock in the first place. His lower body had stiffened up dramatically before the game. He thought an injection would free him up – and it did, for a day or two. Then the pain and stiffness returned worse than before.

'It's as if I did weights for the first time in a year and instead of easing myself in I spent two hours pumping,' he explains. 'The back, the hips and the legs – they're all aching. I have no flexibility at all.'

He's lost weight too. And there's not a hope he'll make the Cork game. By now he's thoroughly exasperated. Truth be told, he's wondering if there's another year of football left in him at all.

'That's the way I'm feeling now,' he says. 'I've given so long and we haven't reached where we wanted to. And sure we have no chance either. They'll say we blew it against London in the league, and we did, but sure how can you prepare a team with the shite that goes on in this county? Three weeks of club hurling before we play Cork and we're expected to go out and compete with the third-best side in Ireland. I don't know if I could face going through all that again.

'It's like we can get it together for the league but when every other county is preparing for the championship and getting a buzz from it, we're walking on eggshells. The arse has fallen out of the whole thing. There's no point in saying otherwise.

'You can't blame the lads in charge of the team. Look at them and the work they're putting in, trying to organise games against Clare and London. I'll tell you what those games were – they were a reminder that we have a match against Cork. Nothing else. They just reminded us what was ahead. Sure most of us haven't seen each other for a month. I couldn't be bothered going through all that again.

'People will say we only have ourselves to blame. I accept we did ourselves serious damage in London but it wasn't because anyone was taking the piss. And I defy anyone to point the finger at us – because we got back on track when we came home.

'The problem is the county board and the way they run their fixtures. Why couldn't we have club football games played before the Cork game? Because that would have made sense, that's why. I'll be doing serious thinking but right now the appetite wouldn't be there for next season, that's for sure.'

As for his medical condition, one early indication from the medics is that it might require a weekly injection into his stomach for five years.

'I don't want to get too worked up about whatever I have until they tell me for sure,' he says. 'But I wouldn't really like to have to do that, to be honest. It's frustrating. It kind of crept up on me. I wouldn't mind if it crept away as quickly as it arrived.'

As Ahearne makes his way into the clubhouse, the rest of the players are trickling out and preparing to leave. Without delay. It's a sombre changing room. Now they fully realise the enormity of the challenge they face against Cork. The bookies have them to be beaten by 14 points. Let's not call a spade a trowel: they'll be doing well to keep it to that.

The players and management thought they had hit rock bottom in Ruislip. Apparently, it can get worse.

Chapter 14
Cork Come Strutting

The Flame Flickers

———•———

May 22, Fraher Field, Dungarvan
Final training session before the Cork game

It's 7.05 p.m., two nights before the start of the football championship, and the sense of anticipation all around County Waterford is palpable. Actually . . . it's not. No one gives a continental hoot down here.

All over Ireland other players are on the physio's table or the training ground – getting a deep massage, stretching limbs, lining up frees, fine-tuning the handpass. With the biggest game of their season fast approaching, most footballers will be already going through their routines half an hour before training officially starts.

In Waterford, though, they march to a different drum.

Officially there's 25 minutes to the start of training, and save for Shane Briggs, the ground is deserted. Presently he's joined by Cillian O'Keeffe, Stephen Cunningham and Wayne Hennessy, but there's no sense that the Munster championship is nigh. And there's definitely no tension in the air, unless you count a couple of PR executives wandering around the pitch and bickering over where to position the sponsors' logos.

There is word tonight, though, that Shane Walsh and Gary Hurney are back, which is something. The downside is it means two others who have worked hard all season will be dropped – and that's never good for morale.

For example, that promising young corner-back Stephen Prendergast has been relegated to the juniors and his response has been to pack it in altogether. It's hard to blame him. He showed immense potential at times in recent months but it hasn't happened for him. In another county he might have been persuaded to stick with it, but here the incentives are fewer and drop-outs are harder to coax back. One or two other players have it in mind to travel abroad over the summer but haven't made it public knowledge yet.

Of course sympathy for those cast adrift does not change the hard reality for the manager. If you were Kiely, you too would be inclined to pragmatism – he's simply looking for his best players. And while Sunday will be all about damage limitation, having the likes of Hurney and Walsh available is a plus.

Unfortunately, it emerges the day before the showdown with Cork that the pair of them had to train with Davy Fitzgerald's senior hurlers three times in the previous 24 hours. You can imagine what state they'll be in.

With numbers depleted, Kiely recalls the veteran Andy Hubbard to the squad. Hubbard, a forward of some note, had been with the team for 13 years but retired in 2008 – or so he thought. He has three weeks' training under his belt and Kiely hopes his experience will settle the other lads. Eamon Walsh, who was on the team that won the Munster U-21 title in 2003, also gets called up.

As the players arrive and tog out it's clear they fear the worst from Conor Counihan's team. In fact they've been far from gung-ho for days now, something that prompted a worried Kiely to take midweek action – in a bid to raise morale, he asked the Fraher Field groundsman, Ollie Drummy, to give a short team talk. It was a demonstration of Jackson's penchant for bringing motivational speakers in from left field – in this instance literally.

Ollie had backed a few winning horses the same day and was in rare old form. In the middle of an epic speech, however, he got the Cork manager, Conor Counihan, mixed up with Ireland's best-loved sportswriter.

'Wait till I tell ye,' he said. 'Cork were here training for two hours during the week and their manager, Con Houlihan, came over to me and asked me to put Cork on top of Waterford on the scoreboard. I told him I wouldn't. Then he came over and asked me what way the wind would be blowing on Sunday. I told him I wasn't a feckin' weatherman. Jaysus, lads, all I can say is they're taking this game shocking seriously.'

It did the trick. At least for a few hours, Ollie put a smile back on everyone's face.

At this stage Kiely is sick of going over old ground and has no desire to slate the county board for the hand he has been dealt. In interviews during the week he chose to talk about a lengthening injury roster rather than the fact he has one hand permanently tied behind his back when trying to prepare a team for such a huge game.

'I'd rather just focus on the game now,' he sighs. 'Sure I knew what was coming. There's no point in getting bogged down by it.'

No point indeed, especially when there are people who are trying hard to map out a better future for football and hurling in Waterford. One of them is the newly-appointed county board secretary, Timmy O'Keeffe, father of Cillian and a former county footballer himself.

He's just been elected the county's first ever full-time secretary, and part of his brief is to sort out domestic fixtures. But that doesn't mean he is sworn to discriminate in favour of the football fraternity.

'I don't accept the argument that the county board fixtures stopped guys from training,' he says. 'The Waterford hurlers trained every Monday night throughout the local hurling championship games – there was nothing to stop the county footballers training either. It's not the county board's fault that they didn't train. My job is to run the fixtures off properly.

'Three times in the last four to five years we failed to have representatives in the Munster football championship,' he adds. 'The 2008 county final was played way too late. I was brought in to restructure things on that front and I will make sure the fixtures are run off properly. I can guarantee you we will have a representative in the Munster club championship in 2009.'

He can see the other side of the coin, though.

'Maybe things could have been done differently this year,' he admits. 'Maybe we could have had one round of club football games before the lads played Cork. But I got very little time to implement that. The fact of the matter is that we're a dual county and we have two groups of six teams that must play five rounds of the hurling championship. We have three rounds to play in the football equivalent.

'There are a couple of problems that need looking at . . . but I won't have people going around pointing the finger of blame at us all the time. The footballers had a great chance to get promoted and they didn't make it. They could have trained away every week while the club hurling was going on but they didn't. It can't all be our fault.'

Out on the field and away from the boardroom, training starts with some light drills, a series of passing movements and then some shooting practice. But intensity is conspicuous by its absence. Mick O'Loughlin, not for the first time, demonstrates his worth by encouraging the players to get more involved and reminding them of the damning stats from the last two games.

'Do that against Cork and they'll murder you,' he warns, as one player butchers a routine drill.

The session winds down after a quick run-out and then it's inside to the showers and afterwards a feed of lasagne.

Tom Condon goes around and hands each player two tickets for Sunday's game, courtesy of the GAA. One or two ask if he can spare an extra one or two, and he doesn't hesitate to hand them over. Condon has been here a thousand times and yet even he looks a little nervous.

'Ah, this is the time I hate most,' he whispers. 'Naming of the team. It always means bad news for someone and that's definitely the case this time round.'

Kiely calls out the starting 15 and it's soon clear the bad news Condon hinted at is the dropping of Ogle, who is understandably disappointed.

Strangely, there's a distinct lack of tension in the room. It's as if they're beaten long before they go out. Jackson throws another curve ball – and again your long-suffering correspondent is on the receiving end.

'There's a lad following ye around all year,' he says, 'and now I'm going to ask him what he thinks.'

This time I see it coming and return serve. It bounces on the line and the crowd applaud.

'Lads, ye've been great to me. Thanks for all the help and every best wish on Sunday.'

Jackson looks disappointed as the players clap my brief message of support.

'I thought you'd say more than that,' he moans.

I fix him with the severest frown I can muster, hoping he will get the message, and finally he does. He moves on and speaks about the need for passion.

'There's a journalist in Cork who wrote today that ye'd be beaten by 23 points,' he says. 'There was a time when I'd be mad over stuff like that but not anymore. It's up to ye to prove that shit wrong.'

He offers final tactical instructions. Gary Hurney on Graham Canty, Brian Wall on John Miskella and Ger Power on Ger Spillane.

'Five of them played us in the junior championship a few years back,' he adds. 'They're a good team but they haven't always done it when the pressure is on. Lads, we've done enough talking by now. There's no pressure on us – is there, Liam?'

Liam Lawlor takes the baton.

'We're completely written off. What's happened here in the past few weeks has been a shambles but we'll draw a line under that now. We have to go out there on Sunday and prove we're intercounty standard. But we'll be doing it for ourselves and our families, no one else really – we don't want them embarrassed, lads.

'We have to show that we can match these fellows. They're good, but show them no fucking respect. They're only another group of men. Lads, it's a football match, not life or death. I think we have to enjoy it. This is why we train hard in the winter. There's no point in us being nervous as kittens.'

Mick Ahearne strikes the same note.

'Who gives a fuck if we lose, lads? Honestly, who gives a fuck? Sure no one is expecting any different. But I think that if we go out there and just throw the kitchen sink at them, not give two hoots about what happens, and play with abandon, we can prove a point. If we get all wound up we'll get destroyed, lads. At the end of the day, enjoy it – one of the best teams in Ireland coming to Fraher Field. Jesus, lads, soak it up.'

Maurice O'Gorman just reminds his men that it's the biggest game of the year and he seems to be one of the few who thinks they can actually win. He speaks briefly before handing back to his manager.

By now the talking is all done. Before they leave, Paul McLoughlin hands out a training schedule for the next four weeks.

'Win or lose on Sunday, we'll have another game to play, lads,' he reminds them. 'But this time we'll prepare to the best of our ability in the hope that we can win that game, whether it's the next round or the qualifiers.

'Lads, this time ye will have to take responsibility for your attendance in training. In other counties players are standing up and refusing to leave their county team's training sessions. We need ye to do the same for four weeks.

'Ye are intercounty players. Clubs should give way to us for the championship. If we are to have any hope of winning a game we need ye to stand up and shout "STOP" to them. To say "No, I'm not fucking going club hurling training or playing a challenge match – I'm a Waterford footballer and I'm training with them". Four weeks. That's all I ask. Are ye with me?'

They nod in assent and head for the hills, resigned to the fact that they will be cannon fodder in just two days' time.

It's sad that they're written off before a ball is kicked and sadder still that they've had to prepare like incompetents. As they disappear in their vans and cars you cannot but respect them for keeping the show on the road. The flame may flicker from time to time – but they haven't let it go out yet.

Lord above, you'd have to admire them.

Princes and Paupers

*24 May, Fraher Field, Dungarvan, County Waterford: Waterford v Cork.
GAA Munster football championship quarter-final*

A tale of princes and paupers. Consider the remoteness of Waterford's chance today and imagine what it must have been like 25 years ago when they were a complete laughing stock. Today, at least, they have some modest status.

A bus pulls up and the Cork lads hop off, togged out, each with a steely glare in the eyes. They're ready for a kill.

Each has his own routine for counting down the minutes; some flick through iPods, some sip water, others pace the pitch before they warm up. They look armed and dangerous, none more so than their inspirational leader, Graham Canty. 'Do not come anywhere near me' is written all over his face.

What you notice most is their sheer physicality. They are not the skinny lightweights of some years ago. It looks like they've spent the winter power-lifting. Their shoulders are broad and square, faces lean, leg muscles rippling. Primed, they crowd into the seething heat of the dressing room. It's a scorching day in Dungarvan, the first of summer, and the Rebels are in the mood.

Since January, most counties have been working towards this, having identified Championship Day as their focal point. But not so Waterford. They targeted the league; promotion was their All-Ireland. They failed in that quest and they've been going through the motions since. If they had drawn Clare, Limerick or Tipperary in the first round of the Munster championship things would have been different; they might have made a bigger push. But Cork? No thanks. Not a prayer. It's only a matter of how much they get beaten by. Can they keep it respectable?

One look around the changing room tells you they're not really up for this. They sit togged out, some with legs crossed, others with legs outstretched. They look like lads sitting in a pub, chatting over a pint.

The contrast between the sides could not be greater. Cork are all serious intent. Their backroom team bustle in and out with lists of things to do. It's like a Monday morning in the office – everyone keen to make a dent in the week's work.

Meanwhile, it's Friday afternoon in the Waterford camp. They look like they are just counting down the clock.

Tony Grey looks anxious though. He's making his championship debut today and he's worked hard to get here. He walks around the dressing room, shirt off, full of nervous energy. It's a big day for him and he doesn't want to be caught out.

Players enquire about what end of the field they'll be warming up at – but no one is quite sure. They nibble jaffa cakes while they await final instructions.

The Waterford juniors trudge in, red-faced and licking their wounds. They've just been hammered by Cork and it's no surprise – their preparation has been even more of a shambles than that of the seniors, if that is possible.

As they take refuge in their changing room the Cork chairman, Jerry O'Sullivan, father of Diarmuid, who this week retired from intercounty hurling, walks down to offer a word of encouragement. But he takes a wrong turn and walks into the senior room by mistake. He is just about to console them when he twigs his error. Jackson starts laughing. The writing is on the wall.

'Oh sorry, lads. John, I'm certainly not tempting fate here,' O'Sullivan winces as he slips out.

It's 3 p.m., 30 minutes away from throw-in and Jackson makes his move. He walks in and shuts the door, aware that it's hot and sticky inside and they're better off in the fresh air. The match stewards have given him five minutes to get his team out on the pitch in any case. He clutches a few notes and flicks through the match programme as he delivers his last speech.

'Lads, the entire country is expecting Cork to beat the living shit out of ye. Your own county is expecting it. But I know ye won't let me down. When it comes to these big championship games ye never do. There are players on this team that would make the Cork side. I have no doubt about that, and I have full confidence in ye.

'A few years back we went down to Kerry and the world expected us to get beaten by 30 points. We missed a penalty in the second half to take the lead and they only beat us by a few points.

'Some of ye have beaten these guys at underage and many more have played with them in college – ye know what they're about. These guys are looking to win an All-Ireland title but they're only down here to blow ye away. I know ye won't let that happen.'

He goes through the team one more time and issues last-minute instructions until the stewards knock on the door and tell Timmy O'Keeffe it's time to mosey on out.

Paul McLoughlin offers the last word.

'Keep your discipline, lads. Don't get sucked in. Track your marker and have a go at him. I'll tell ye one thing – a few weeks back ye nearly beat Sligo in their own backyard. Two years ago they won the Connacht title and the pace of our game with them was as good as any championship match.

'I'm telling ye, lads, ye can rattle this Cork team. But your attitudes have to be right. There's no point in a fella getting frustrated, getting sent off and leaving us a man down. That's cowardly stuff and I don't want to see it.

'Hit them fair and hard, leave your mark, run at them and give them something to think about. If ye're bollixed, suck in the air and go again. It's only a game of football, lads – go out there and give it everything ye have.'

Outside, the Cork secretary, Frank Murphy, stands in the centre of the pitch with a handful of documentation as the players warm up in front of him. He's just come out the other side of the third players' strike of his reign but it hasn't taken a feather out of him. You just wonder what the most recent dispute achieved. Sure, Gerald McCarthy got the bullet, but it was Frank the players wanted out. But there he is, on the field, as if nothing ever happened.

There are 3,500 souls in the crowd. It's reasonable to assume not even 500 are from Waterford. There are red flags, hats and scarves all over the place. To all appearances, Cork are the home team.

Fair to say this game hasn't caught the imagination of the Waterford public. In another county the sunshine would have brought a sizeable walk-up crowd – here it has sent them to the beach at Tramore.

A Bright Start

Nonetheless, the home side take the game to Cork. For 10 minutes they throw the proverbial kitchen sink, linking up brilliantly as they surge forward. They find great dividends in attacking the left flank of Cork's defence, and they manufacture five scoring chances in those 10 minutes.

Sadly, it's the year-long malaise – they manage to convert only one of those chances. Brian Wall clips over a free but they hit four shocking wides. And though Cork look briefly like a rabbit caught in the headlights, they trail by only a point. Imagine the shockwaves had Kiely's men stormed five points clear.

Inevitably, the visitors come hunting and, just to show the gulf in class, Donncha O'Connor gets three touches of the ball and scores 1-2 in seven minutes.

It's probably generous to credit the goal to him because technically it comes off Wayne Hennessy and would have gone down as an own goal in soccer. It's a horrible, scuttery score to give away – and it rips the stomach out of the home side.

By the end of the half Waterford still haven't managed to score from play, but in injury time they tack on two points to make the scoreline some way respectable; it's 1-9 to 0-3 at the break.

They are far from despondent. The truth is they have done OK. Thomas O'Gorman, for example, was given the job of marshalling the highly-gifted James Masters. Four balls went in between the two of them and O'Gorman won all four. They switched Masters to the corner, off the tigerish twin, and he grabbed two points. So Kiely moved O'Gorman back on the Cork dangerman and Masters didn't get a look-in again.

Maurice O'Gorman, meanwhile, looked after Pierce O'Neill, an All-Star and International Rules player, and didn't yield an inch either.

Leaving the own goal aside, Hennessy is having a stormer and Hurney looks like he could cut loose at any minute. So – despite the score and despite the fact Cork have so many resources, so many dangermen – it's a pretty upbeat Waterford dressing room at half-time.

The players are melting with the heat, though. Liam Ó Líonáin, who has worked hard in defence but just hasn't got going up front, whips off his gear and goes under a cold shower. Fluids are gulped down, players take toilet breaks and there are huddles around the room as they try to dissect the 35 minutes just passed.

'Lads, the scoreline makes it look bad but ye know it's not bad,' McLoughlin says. 'Your performance has been very encouraging. But the one target I'm going to set ye is to add more to our scoring tally. We need that for whatever game we play next. Hit them with a couple of early scores and rattle them. I guarantee you they think this game is over. Hit them early and let's get some respectability on the scoreboard. That's important, boys. Ye deserve it.'

Kiely takes over.

'Ye absolutely owned the ball for the first 10 minutes and even up till the end we had some lovely passages of play. We're just lacking a few scores. Go for it, lads. There's nothing else to say. Sure ye're not afraid of them, ye showed that . . . that Cork team have dished out several hammerings over the years but they're lucky to be nine points ahead of us, lads.'

Hurney offers the parting shot.

'That was great play, lads, but let's use the head up front. If we do we can give them plenty to think about.'

A Respectable Scoreline

They march out for the second half in surprisingly upbeat mood and proceed to tear at Cork for the remainder of the game. Several times they run through the Cork half-back line, Maurice O'Gorman, Ó Líonáin and Hurney exposing frailties that must have been of special interest to the watching Kerry manager, Jack O'Connor.

In fact, it takes three brilliant saves to spare Cork severe embarrassment, their powerfully-built goalkeeper, Alan Quirke, denying Ó Líonáin once and Hurney twice when goals seemed certain.

But Quirke cannot prevent Shane Walsh scoring a beauty. Maurice O'Gorman goes on one of his mazy runs and is fouled 30 yards out. Brian Wall walks over to take the free but Walsh rips the ball from his hands and lets fly. It rattles the net.

Respectability, at least.

At the other end, however, the scores keep on coming and by the time the final whistle sounds Cork have won easily, 2-18 to 1-7.

It's amazing the different reactions you get as the players leave the field. Eddie Rockett flashes a rueful smile as he walks off the pitch. 'That was some fucking shambles,' he says.

Paul Ogle, who came on during the second half, looks like he's about to hit someone. Ó Líonáin just casts his eyes to the heavens.

Tom Wall is disgusted. 'We could have got another 3-7 there,' he sighs.

Maybe he's not wrong. But this 14-point beating is not the end of the world. Much worse was feared and predicted. Cork have beaten most teams in the land this year and stand two divisions above Waterford.

'There's something to work on for the qualifiers now,' Mick O'Loughlin says.

'Bloody right,' Paul McLoughlin agrees. 'We've given them a training schedule for the next few weeks. If we stick to that and get a half-decent draw we can win a game in this championship yet.'

Jackson, of course, will look only at the positives.

'Jesus, there were times when a few of our lads tore at them and they simply had no answer to us. The O'Gormans were actually able to solo the ball better than some of the Cork lads. We have as much football in us as anyone else but sure our build-up was poor and it didn't help. Overall, though, it could have been a lot worse.'

The positives? Walsh hit one of the best goals he will ever score; himself and Hurney were excellent, which is remarkable considering they were made to train four times with the county hurlers in the two days before this match. Crazy.

But back to the game and the plus points. Today the O'Gormans were simply imperious and at times the rest of the team linked well as they surged forward.

There were the usual negatives. Their shooting was awful; it has actually worsened during the year. And most unusually for Waterford, they conceded two soft goals. It's been a while since they did that.

In the dressing room, a challenge game against Tipperary on 16 June is announced – at least it will give them some sort of focus.

Word then comes through that Limerick have just caused a massive shock by beating Tipperary in the other Munster opener. So it's clear both Tipperary and Waterford have plenty of work on their hands.

With that they leave for home. It's to the qualifiers now, their last hope of salvaging something from the season. Something to banish memories of the 2009 Munster championship.

Chapter 15
Dreams May Crumble

Missing in Australia

12 June, Stradbally, County Laois

After two weeks in Sydney, Ger Power is back home and glad to be. It wasn't a pleasant trip or anything of the sort.

On 10 May 2009, Seán Walsh, the brother of Ger's girlfriend, Bríd, disappeared in Australia. Seán is 26, a biomedical engineer, and by all accounts he had the world at his feet. One night he just vanished. The alarm was raised and Bríd has been in Sydney since, looking for her brother. Ger says she has been playing a blinder, searching everywhere and raising awareness of the matter.

Just hours after playing against Cork in the Munster championship, Power went to join the search party. While the rest of his team were hitting the town for the night, drowning their sorrows and thinking of what might have been, he caught a plane and flew Down Under. There wasn't much he could do but offer support. Still, he didn't need to think twice about it.

'Bríd and her sister, Mairéad, have done absolutely everything you could imagine and there was nothing for me to do except be there,' he explains. 'I stayed behind to play against Cork and then flew to Sydney the night of that game. Bríd's brother-in-law Declan travelled out with me. I was glad of the company.

'The thing is, Seán was due to come back home to Waterford the day after he disappeared and it's been really tough on his family – they're wicked close. They don't have a clue what happened, there's been no inkling whatsoever, and that's hard to accept.

'His parents have flown out to Sydney now and my heart goes out to them, but while there is hope they have something, I suppose.'

From home and from farther afield the Walsh girls have done everything possible to find Seán. They set up a website, which received tens of thousands of hits. They blitzed the Australian media and even appeared on a 'missing persons' show live on television. They tapped into the electronic media and set up Twitter and Facebook accounts. Two sisters doing all they can to ease the worry of their parents. Two sisters trying to get their brother back.

Ger stayed in the background and tried to be positive. The girls had all the angles covered but they knew he was there if needed.

'A lot of the time I was just sitting around, waiting to help the girls but they honestly had every lead followed up,' Ger adds. 'They actually could not have done any more. They were delighted that we went over because these are rough times and the girls know that this might only be the beginning. At the start you fear the worst but there's just been no sign of anything. So you cling onto the hope that he might come back.'

As with so many missing persons, there is no explanation. Weeks after the disappearance Power is still struggling to make sense of it all.

'Seán is a highly qualified man, an intelligent and successful professional, and he was very popular as well. He had lots of friends and was a big hit with the women too – there are a few devastated girls over there. He had absolutely nothing to hide. The lad was easygoing and hugely involved in the GAA scene in Sydney as well.'

Something else Power struggles to comprehend is the fact that 13,000 people go missing in New South Wales every year. 'It's just a crazy statistic,' he says, shaking his head.

One of the most popular members of the Waterford team, Power has a lovely manner about him, and you can see how his calm, genial nature would be a great comfort to Bríd and the rest of the Walsh family. He readily admits that coming back to the team has been a blessing, a temporary distraction from endlessly mulling over Seán's possible fate.

'It was brilliant to come back to the lads,' he asserts. 'I think if I hadn't the GAA I would crack up. I'd be working on the farm all day and wouldn't have the release of playing hurling or football. Coming back to the boys on the team and having the craic in the dressing room again was a release – you'd miss all that. The lads are brilliant; they were very supportive when I was away. They wouldn't say much about things but they'd let you know they'd do anything to help.

'It's the same with Jackson. When he moves on, people will be quick to say that we let him down by not getting promotion and, yeah, we're very disappointed over that. He has been very loyal to me, and you feel like you owe him one. But you feel the same about your teammates. In the past few weeks I have learned that when our team does run its course and when the likes of Mick Ahearne and Wayne Hennessy and the lads move on, it's only then that the arse will fall out of Waterford football.

'I mean that. If you are a kid, everything here is geared towards hurling from the age of 11 upwards and football championships are only played to get them out of the way. I've been doing a lot of thinking about it. People might have us down as 'nearly men' but the way I see it, when our group moves on we're in big trouble.'

Power is right. It's hard to see where the transfusion of new blood will come from. For now he'll help keep the show on the road. And he'll continue to hope the Walsh family will soon get the good news they crave.

Back to the Training Ground

—•—

13 June, Fraher Field, Dungarvan, County Waterford

Paul Ogle strides toward the front exit of Fraher Field and feels like letting loose.

Only nine players bothered to make it to training tonight. Nine. For a competition in which they might feasibly claim a scalp. The qualifiers could of course see them pitted hopelessly against the likes of Armagh or Donegal, but the draw could just as easily throw up Leitrim, Clare, London or Tipperary – teams against which they would back themselves.

Yet there's been shocking indifference since the Cork game. Players are back with their clubs. Brian Wall, Liam Lawlor and Patrick Hurney have been called up to the Waterford intermediate hurling team. Others have just decided to take a week or two off.

Their championship campaign looks increasingly like a lost cause, but much blood, sweat and tears have been invested in this squad over the years – the men behind them won't give up easily.

Mick O'Loughlin gets on his mobile and taps out another group text message. 'One last push. Shoulders to the wheel.' Call it a word of encouragement, a warning, an order or just an old-fashioned plea – but those few words seem to work. Players are reminded there's little point training all year just to blow it now.

So they meet again a night later and this time 18 turn out. They are informed that the forthcoming challenge match with Tipperary is next up on the agenda and so they have a focus again.

'That's what we need or else it's curtains,' Ogle states. 'People might reckon that because we were one of the first teams out of the championship we'd have plenty of time to get ready for the qualifiers.

'That's not the case. In the three sessions we've had since the Cork game, there have been attendances of 9, 18 and 12 players. Our lads are dragged left, right and centre and we don't know who we're playing next, which

189

doesn't help.

'I don't like sob stories but look at my schedule as an example. I've played four matches in the last six days. It was the exact same story last season – I played 13 games in 8 days. That must be some sort of a record. Jesus, even a Premiership soccer player wouldn't play more than twice in one week; they'd be rested. And now I have to get a scan on a suspected fracture in my foot, the result of so many games.

'But down here this is an annual thing. Get a rake of club games played before the Waterford hurlers kick off the championship and we won't have sight nor sound of a club game for the summer until the hurlers get knocked out. Then there'll be the usual rush to get games played off before Christmas.

'That's our lot but we move on. We can blame the board for this mess, the management for not standing up to them – but we the players have to look at ourselves too. Simple as that. We owe it to the team to lift the numbers at training.

'At the end of the day the fact we lost to London will give the board a get-out clause. People have an excuse to bad-mouth us, so if we make noises about the preparation we've had, we'll be shot down.

'But people forget very quickly. Not so long ago the Waterford hurlers were in the same boat – they lost to Kerry in 1993. Only for the fact that everyone rowed in together and got them out of that mess they might still be in trouble. It shows what can be done with co-operation. All we need is a bit of extra effort and we'll get promoted or win a qualifier. And that would be a start.'

As Fraher Field empties for the night, O'Loughlin, the team trainer, makes another pertinent point.

'While 18 players turned up the other night and put in a very good effort, you could see how their fitness levels have dropped since the end of the league. Hurling for your club bears no relation to playing football for your county. And the problem is that the backroom team really have no say in

190

organising our preparations – we're totally at the mercy of the board and the clubs. The players are pulled in all directions. Until they stand up and realise that they're intercounty men and start saying "No" when it comes to playing Mickey Mouse league challenges for their clubs, we're at nothing.'

Meanwhile, the early rounds of the GAA championships continue. And though they're nowhere to be seen, the Waterford footballers are nonetheless able to take solace from several results.

Cork destroy Kerry in the Munster semi-final replay. James Masters, kept in his box by Thomas O'Gorman a few weeks earlier, rules the roost as Cork ease through by eight points. They had beaten Jackson's men by only six points more.

A day later in the Leinster championship Wicklow bring Westmeath to extra time before losing by only three points. They miss a penalty and squander chances to win the game. Had they won, they would have played in front of a full house in Croke Park at the end of June. This is the team Waterford drew with a few months ago.

Up north comes the biggest shock of all. At the end of the league, Waterford trotted out their second team to play Antrim and led by five points as the fringe players got game time. Now Antrim, thanks to inspirational displays from Paddy Cunningham and Thomas McCann, have knocked Donegal out of the championship and will lock horns with Cavan in the Ulster semi-final.

Those three results bring no tangible rewards for the Waterford men – just a little more light at the end of the tunnel. One small break and they might be off on a run – like Limerick or Wexford, who rose from the lower divisions after a couple of decent results.

There's also solace to be found in the fact that the Waterford hurlers struggled badly in their Munster semi-final, drawing with Limerick in possibly the worst game since the invention of the sliotar. John Mullane apart, the Waterford attack was dire, and yet Gary Hurney got only about six minutes of action after playing in every league game.

Hurney deserved more than a few minutes and he may well be sick of the bench by now. If it's actual game time he's looking for he knows which door to knock on.

Maybe it's fantasy stuff but there's a sense that if they can get a half-decent draw in the qualifiers these guys could yet have a sharp sting in their tail.

Putting It Up to Tipp and Wexford

15 June, Dr Morris Park, Thurles, County Tipperary

John Evans is animated, cajoling his young Tipperary side to invest more energy in their warm-up, but if he thinks his team lacks urgency he should see the Waterford dressing room. All they are lacking are pipes and slippers. It looks like they are winding down for the night instead of getting themselves up for this challenge match, and the mother and father of all beatings could be on the cards.

Tipperary go through their pre-match drills in custom-made training gear, their names on the back of their shirts. It's another indication of how far Waterford are lagging behind. For 10 years little has separated the two teams, but fresh from successive promotions Tipperary are aiming for the heights, leaving their old foes stuck in the mire.

While Tipp work up a sweat 15 minutes before throw-in, Kiely's lads chat among themselves about the weekend just passed. The day before, Patrick Hurney was the star of the show for the county intermediate hurlers against Limerick. Brian Wall and Liam Lawlor played too, so they're tired and hardly in the mood for another game tonight. But there is little choice – bodies are in short supply.

Thomas O'Gorman phones from work in Wexford to say he won't make it in time. Maurice cries off with an injury minutes before throw-in. There's still no sign of Mick Ahearne returning. He has lost more weight and is still having tests. His teammates are praying he will be okay. Liam Ó Líonáin has a torn quad. Wayne Hennessy is playing a club hurling game with Ardmore – management are furious.

In all there are 18 players available but after a run of club games they're nursing ankles, holding shoulders and rubbing backs.

At the far end of Dr Morris Park, Declan Carr trains the Tipperary U-21 hurlers and the ground buzzes with activity on a lovely summer's evening.

Eventually the Waterford boys are coaxed out of the dressing room and they do a brief warm-up. The game starts and – wouldn't you know it – they proceed to boss Tipperary all around the park. Straightaway you can see Stephen Cunningham is the man with the biggest cause. He feels he should have started against Cork. Most of his teammates agree. And you can see why. He belies his years with an action-packed display, cruising from flank to flank and from end to end. There's no doubt about it – he'll have to start in the qualifiers.

Glen Kelly gets a rare start in goal, and his booming kick-outs give the team every chance of breaking ball and surging into attack. Brian Phelan and Michael O'Gorman step up to the mark, as does Conor McGrath, a player Kiely rates highly but also one with plenty to prove.

Paul Ogle is handed a midfield role and appointed free-taker in Brian Wall's absence. He plays his best football of the past two months. Tony Grey and Patrick Hurney are rampant in front of him.

In short, you just can't figure this team out – they are utterly unpredictable.

Leading by three points, they gather for the half-time huddle.

'Don't let this slip,' Ogle warns. 'We didn't travel all the way over here to have the piss taken or to get beaten. We're on top, we're well on top and let's keep it that way.'

They make their way back onto the pitch and take up positions. Kiely hands Tom Wall the number one shirt in place of Kelly, and as Wall moves toward the posts, Jackson subtly transmits his tactical plan to his keeper.

'Hey, Tom,' he booms across the pitch for all to hear. 'Hit every single kick-out on top of Brian Phelan – he's winning them all.'

Spectators laugh heartily. No codebreaker is needed to decipher that gameplan.

Nonetheless, Waterford ram home their advantage and cruise to a five-point lead. Evans looks baffled; Tipp weren't expecting this.

As usual, though, Waterford let it slip. A long, speculative ball is played into their defence. Wall comes to collect but spills it. It's poked into the net. It's game even – and time is about up.

There are groans in the visiting camp. Then Wall redeems the situation with a quick kick-out that finds Cunningham, who sets up another attack. Hurney and Michael O'Gorman combine to feed Ger Power, who smashes the ball to the net with his left foot. After all he's been through lately it's great that Power is the man who wins the game.

The final whistle blows. They have won by three points when a hiding was very much on the cards.

'That was fucking brilliant but we can't let our lads know that or they'll get carried away,' Paul McLoughlin remarks to Jackson as he strides across to the players. He addresses them in less-than-ecstatic tones.

'That was okay, lads, but it wasn't great either. We have plenty to work on, so we'll meet again for training on Friday night. Now are we going to see you all there? Are ye going to be man enough to turn up? Because let's hear it now if you're not.

'We have a good chance of winning a game in the qualifiers but only if we prepare. And we can only prepare if ye have the balls to stand up to your clubs. Ye're fucking intercounty players – I'm sick of saying it to ye. We need ye. We need ye Friday night.'

They warm down and compliment each other on a good evening's work.

Meanwhile, Evans keeps his Tipp team in a huddle for about 20 minutes.

'Not only did ye not win the 50-50 balls, ye didn't even win the 70-30 balls,' he berates them.

Earlier in the year it looked like Tipp were taking the quickest possible route to the top but lately they've lost some of their footing. Still, there's little doubt the Kerryman will soon have them back on high ground. What he's achieved with them so far has been astounding.

While Kiely waits to greet Evans, he sums up the evening: 'Food for thought. At last we finished out a game that we deserved to win. It's been a while since we did that.'

The players head off to the Park Avenue Hotel for a steak, tired but reasonably happy. Most of them have racked up two matches and three training sessions in seven days. Their limbs are weary. But at least they have something to fight for again.

'The show's back on the road,' Cunningham says as he walks to his car, a contented smile creasing his features. 'It's nice to have a bit of hope again.'

Maurice O'Gorman hears him. 'Ah, if it's one thing we have down here it's hope,' he says softly.

'We'll always have that.'

* * *

21 June, Walsh Park, Waterford City, County Waterford

The Wexford tour bus pulls up at 10.30 a.m. and its contents are quickly unloaded as from a conveyor belt. We're talking exercise bikes, cones, nets, training gear, footballs, energy drinks and flip charts.

Presently, some 15 cars arrive and the Wexford players hop out. They put in a training session 90 minutes before their challenge match with Waterford is scheduled to throw in. They have 34 players at their disposal and their manager, Jason Ryan, is directing operations.

Wexford reached the All-Ireland semi-final in 2008, but they were blown out of the Leinster championship in 2009 by Kildare just a week ago. They have much to do to get back on track. It looks like classic second-season syndrome.

The Waterford lads, meanwhile, stroll in at their ease. Most of them are in the dressing room by about 11.30 a.m. They look out at their opponents swarming all over the place. They can't get over the exercise bike at all.

'You'd have some job getting our lads up on that,' laughs Ger Power.

Wexford have the makings of two teams, but Waterford can barely field one. They have just two fit subs, including Seán O'Hare, who trained with the county U-21 hurlers a few hours earlier. He's knackered so they rest him. In the stand Maurice O'Gorman, Shane Briggs and Liam Ó Líonáin look on, nursing their injuries.

The sun is blazing down and once more the lads aren't in much form for a warm-up. Apart from O'Hare, the only other reserve on the line is Tom Wall, who has to watch as Glen Kelly starts in goal for the second game in a row.

'I must have done something wrong – I bet you I won't start in the qualifiers,' he says, clearly despondent.

But the boys don't spare him. Kelly makes a spectacular save in the warm-up, and Briggs, always up for mischief, doesn't miss the opportunity.

'Attaboy, Glen! Jesus, I'd say you're one of the best goalies Waterford has ever produced. You're a dead cert for the qualifiers.'

Wall just laughs.

This game is notable for a number of things.

Paul Ogle twists awkwardly in a divot early in the first half and hobbles off. He's just returned from a cruciate-ligament operation, and no one wants to think the worst. But you can tell from his reaction he's in serious strife. In the dressing room he wears a haunted expression. It's the other leg this time and he can read the signs. He's handed crutches and advised to go for a scan. Here we go again. The man is in pieces.

Back outside, Jason Ryan – visibly concerned by his team's decline this season – spends much of the game running to and from the stand trying to inject urgency. Wexford's running off the ball and intensity of tackling are on a different planet from Waterford's, but there are only a couple of points between them at the break.

With 10 minutes left Ryan's team have stretched their lead to seven, but despite looking dead and buried under the scorching midday sun, Waterford somehow raise one last gallop.

Thomas O'Gorman, Tony Grey, Stephen Cunningham and Patrick Hurney lead the charge with points as they claw their way back. With just seconds left the team form an attack down the right flank and after three quick-fire passes the ball pops up in front of Ger Power, who has raced to the edge of the square. His shot almost bursts the rigging – and for the second week in a row he has saved the day. It's a draw, 1-14 apiece.

It may only be a challenge but what a result for Waterford. It sets them up nicely for the qualifier draw that night. They are now riding the wave of two great efforts. Jackson credits their improvement to the fact they've been playing club football – their touch is back.

Dreams May Crumble

That evening, in the comfort of their homes, players and management settle down to watch the draw for the qualifiers. In his own lair Jackson sets the mood by first watching an old video of a West Waterford junior football final.

The man is obsessed with the game. He spends a few minutes chuckling heartily at the commentary provided by Tony Coffey, one of a local group of film-makers. 'Batchelors in Trouble' specialise in comedy inspired by Irish rural life in days of yore. Jackson's been a fan ever since they appeared on *The Late Late Show* nine years ago and left Pat Kenny with quite a mess, literally, on his hands.

'The lads marched into the television studio and they brought an oul donkey with them,' Kiely recalls, shaking with laughter. 'Sure didn't the donkey do a great big shite in the middle of the floor. Quick as a flash one of the lads turned around and said, "Don't worry, folks, there's one for everyone in the audience." It was great stuff altogether.'

He stops laughing and switches off the DVD. TV3 are showing the draw live.

Armagh are pulled out of the hat first and Jackson reckons Waterford are certs to be pitted against them. But . . . it's Monaghan. He breathes a sigh of relief – two strong teams gone there.

One by one, though, Clare, Leitrim, London, Tipperary and even Louth – teams that would be within Waterford's grasp – come out of the hat. The softer draws are fast evaporating.

In the end they get Meath. Away from home. It could have been much kinder.

The reaction is pretty muted. As usual, the manager tries to apply a positive spin by reminding all and sundry that Meath are not the team they used to be. And he's right. But they have Stephen Bray, Brian Farrell, Cian Ward, Joe Sheridan and Anthony Moyles. They're still two divisions above Waterford.

'It's a bad draw,' Ger Power admits frankly. 'We were hoping for the best but it's hard to be optimistic. You learn not to put yourself out there. That way you can't be taken down. We have to be realistic – we're in big trouble. The last time we went up there we were absolutely hammered.

Let's call a spade a spade – we're in big trouble. Christ, we never get a break.'

* * *

28 June, Abbeyside, County Waterford

The big summer show has been underway for two months and Gary Hurney is a part of it.

Well, he was until last week. Waterford are back in the Munster hurling final and Hurney was the man in possession of the Number 14 shirt. Boys Own stuff. Then, last weekend, he broke a collarbone. Season over, or as good as. Just when he looked like making his name.

He's sitting down at home, cursing his luck, flicking through the channels and cursing the fact that the only action he'll get now is watching Wimbledon and maybe the Tour de France on the box. And he's glad there's some bit of sport on TV. He's out of work for the next seven weeks. A self-employed electrician out of action in a recession – it ain't pretty.

By the way, his hurling had improved tenfold under the intense and relentless drills Davy Fitzgerald swears by. He had graduated from the fringes of notching a point or two per game to the fulcrum of the action.

Hitting two fine goals against Cork in the latter stages of the national league threw his name up in lights. After a career carved 'off Broadway', he was starting to think his time in the main theatres had arrived.

'This couldn't have come at a worse stage in the season,' he sighs, only slightly less distraught than his football teammate and fellow injury victim Ogle.

'The Munster hurling final – you dream of playing in one. Then the chance appears and it's taken away just as quick. I think I was a real option for the management. I played against Limerick in the semi-final replay and only got about half a dozen touches of the ball, but still they know what I can do. I was hoping to start the final but it's just fierce disappointing.'

Being the man he is, Hurney was also ready to answer the call for the football qualifier against Meath – despite the game taking place just eight days before the Munster final. That would have produced another tug of war between the two camps but he's his own man and his heart told him playing in Navan was the right thing to do.

When needed against Sligo and Cork he had stepped up to the mark, even if he had to undergo a commando regime in the days before playing Conor Counihan's men.

'Well,' he recalls, 'people were trying to tell Shane Walsh and me we couldn't play and the truth is everyone had an opinion – but we just went along with what we wanted. We played against Galway on the Wednesday before that football match, we played Clare on the Friday and we trained three times on the day before Cork.

'People thought we were nuts – going off to play football the next day but we said nothing, kept our heads down and did what we wanted. We played the football while everyone else was making their minds up for us.

'And you know what? Alan Quirke had to make three great saves that afternoon – we were not 14 points a worse team. I was glad I played. So was Shane.'

While Cork were always in control, the hurling championship gave Hurney another shot at the big time. He got only five minutes in the drawn game with Limerick but that wasn't the worst thing in the world.

On a wild, sodden day, it proved arguably the worst game in the long and glorious history of hurling. Hurney duly started the replay in place of the injured Ken McGrath, fetched a number of balls and helped the team reach the Munster final. That's where the full stop looks to have been placed on his season, though.

'Maybe if we reach an All-Ireland semi or final I could be back in contention but I can't even go for a run for another month,' he says. 'It was just one of those things – I was tackling Michael 'Brick' Walsh in training and accidentally collided with him. The shoulder dropped and I knew it was trouble.

'But I'd like to think I've proven that I can play at this level now – hopefully it won't be my last chance.'

He sits back and makes plans for the weeks ahead. He'll try a session or two on the bike next month and then maybe a light jog. By then, the path to the physio will have been retraced several times and he'll be on the road back to recovery. For the moment, though, he has only two dates in mind. Navan on Saturday night to support his brother, Patrick, and the rest of Jackson's boys. And Thurles a week later for the Munster hurling final, arm in a sling and trying to keep a brave face.

In an ideal world Hurney would be playing in both games, but he knows it doesn't take long for dreams to crumble.

Paul Ogle could testify to that too.

His world is just about to collapse again.

Chapter 16
The Final Act

The Tumour and the Cruciate
— • —

4 July, Poitín Still, County Dublin

The players are stretching in the car park of the popular Rathcoole pub and restaurant, where they have stopped off for a pre-match meal after the long trek from the south-east.

Paul Ogle, hobbling on crutches and wearing a grimace of resignation, is one of the last off the bus. This place holds bad memories for him. It's déjà vu all over again.

Three years ago, they had pulled into the same car park on their way to play Cavan in the national league. As the others lads went inside to tackle the carvery, Ogle called the manager aside and dropped a bombshell: he had a tumour on his neck and needed surgery.

Kiely's reflex was one of shock. 'Jesus, Paul,' he exclaimed – before recognising the need to stay positive: 'Look, I'm sure you'll be fine. You're young and fit and please God you'll be okay. Remember, there'll be a place on this team for you when you come back.'

'What do you mean?' Ogle replied. 'I'm playing against Cavan. And I'm playing in the championship against Kerry in a couple of weeks. I'm getting the operation afterwards. I have it put back until after the matches. I'm playing and I'd die for that jersey.'

The manager took stock, wondering if he'd ever been as impressed by anyone as he was by this guy. One thing was clear: there was no point in arguing the matter.

Ogle played the league game and they denied Cavan promotion. A few weeks later he played against Kerry and they ran them to eight points. That itself was a victory of sorts. He was their best player; RTÉ Radio named him 'man of the match'.

'Looking back, I don't know how I played against Cavan but I suppose I was just focused on winning,' Ogle says. 'I got the operation and the tumour was removed. Since then I've had a few scares along the way. I'm waiting for a few tests now again, but I'm really positive about them.'

Dealing with the diagnosis and subsequent operation required serious mental strength. But tearing his right cruciate ligament in 2008 was no 'lark in the park' either. It robbed him of game time – tantamount to cutting off his oxygen supply.

And when he finally put that episode behind him he could have done without the agony of rupturing the other cruciate the following year. But it's happened. The hits just keep on coming, and the man is almost punch drunk.

You check in with him to see how bad it is and it breaks your heart a little to talk with the guy. He is a gentleman, a man who adores the game. But there's an elephant in the room that will not go away – that dreaded cruciate.

Understandably he's distraught. It's seven days since the challenge game against Wexford and, truth be told, it was only in recent weeks he had rediscovered his old form. Against Tipperary, he was all action, up and down the field, kicking frees for fun. He started against Wexford in the same vein. Then after 10 minutes he caught his left foot in a deep hole. The leg was trapped, dead straight, and as he fell, all the pressure transferred to the side of the knee. He incurred the worst possible type of cruciate injury.

By the following Tuesday he had retraced the familiar route to the Whitfield Clinic, where he had been fast-tracked for an MRI scan. That's where the bad news hit him with the subtlety of a brick in the face. Gone again for another nine months.

'I have to say it was one of the darkest moments in my life,' he says. 'A couple of medical pals pulled a few strings and I got seen to within a few days. I got the initial diagnosis and that night I went down to Tramore to tell my club coaches what happened, but I was in complete denial. I didn't think this could happen again. They asked me to get a second opinion so I went to Waterford Regional Hospital and it turned out the injury is actually worse than initially thought.

'There I was, clinging to the hope that it had been misdiagnosed and it proved to be even worse.'

He's waiting now to see when Dr Tadhg O'Sullivan can operate. He had arranged to travel to the US for two weeks with his fiancée, Dee, to continue preparations for their wedding in the summer of 2010, but he'll have to juggle around the surgeon's schedule.

Right now his life is up in the air. It's an achingly lonely time. At first he was unable to discuss the injury because he was so upset. A week later, while he was still sombre, he was in better form.

He recounted how he went home in tears on the night when the second consultation surpassed his worst fears. He told of how the phone never stopped ringing with messages of support, and though he wasn't in the form to engage with anyone, he was glad of the warmth.

'When I go to sleep at night there are still a few tears but I'm improving,' he admits.

'I suppose the latest setback kind of brought everything home.'

One night he went to his room and pulled out the card his teammates had given him in 2006 when they heard about the tumour. And despite the darkness of his mood he managed a smile. All those same lads had been in touch again – and it lifted him again. A call from teammate and fellow defender John Phelan even got him laughing for the first time since the injury. Then he stopped feeling sorry for himself.

He's already back in the gym and has targeted February 2010, eight months after the rupture, as the date of his next comeback. But he's worried about insurance. His general policy will cover the cost of the operation but he can claim only €200 worth of physio.

Tom Wall had a similar experience three years ago. He broke a finger playing against Antrim and missed seven weeks' work. A self-employed electrician, he filled out umpteen insurance forms but ended up with just €400 in compensation for the entire period he was idle. He was down about €4,500.

Ogle, at least, will have the summer recess from school to recuperate but it's the cost of rehab that worries him.

'The official policy means I can have five visits to the physio,' he says, 'but you'd have that clocked up in the two weeks after the op. It really has me worried, extremely worried actually. You would really need six months of intensive physio on this and further treatment afterwards to avoid complications down the line.

'I just can't accept the fact I'll only be covered for €200. I need to know the county board will support me on this and I've emailed Dessie Farrell in the GPA. I was talking to Dermot Geraghty, who played corner-back for Mayo. He had the same injury but he told me he didn't even have to make a phone call. It was all sorted out for him. I guess that's the difference.'

Right now, though, his immediate worry is making himself invisible in the dressing room as the others fine-tune preparations for the Meath game. Instead of playing midfield he will be confined to speaking to the team beforehand. Kiely has already asked him to say a few words.

'In my mind Paul Ogle is one of the greatest players the GAA has ever known,' the manager explains. 'The day he came to me with the initial bad news in 2006 it broke my heart. But all I have for him is admiration. I don't care, no one else that I know in the GAA has the mental strength he has. If he was from Kerry or Tyrone they would have him worshipped as a hero. Well, the man is a hero.'

Onwards to Navan

The squad have assembled in a back room of the Poitín Still when Ogle takes the floor. He keeps it short; there's no point in getting emotional at this stage.

'Lads, you all know I want to be out there with ye and it's killing me not to play. I had to look on for nine months and now I'll have to do it again. You have to enjoy every minute of it out there, because you don't know when it will be taken away from you.

'Tear at them and don't sit back. We tend to sit back and drop our heads when we concede a few scores. Have a go at them; work them up and down the field. They're not the Meath of old. They'll find it hard to come down from playing in front of 60,000 against Dublin in Croke Park to playing us in Navan on a Saturday evening. I think we're due a big game and I wish you all the best.'

They applaud while Kiely produces a white board with the Meath team mapped out on it. He reminds his players of their tactical duties and offers a thumbnail sketch of every member of the opposition.

There's no point in going overboard. It's a baking hot day and sitting around talking will do them no favours. It's wrapped up pretty quickly and they pile back onto the bus.

Onward to An Uaimh. The final act of their season?

* * *

6 p.m., An Uaimh, Páirc Tailteann, Navan

They've arrived at the ground a tad early but it's hard to time game-day journeys at the best of times. Had they left Waterford 30 minutes later they would have been pushing it to beat the match traffic.

Though this qualifier is most definitely an undercard billing, with nine other top-class games on offer around the country, a decent crowd of about 5,000 have found their way to Páirc Tailteann. But there is no hum of anticipation. The Meath faithful have come to see blood shed. Stung by the collapse against Dublin, they want to see their team bite back with a vengeance.

Under the stand in the dressing room the Waterford players scoff jaffa cakes and sip water. They chat easily, but you detect an edge to their banter – it's like the forced skittishness of men about to face the firing squad.

Oddly, at the same time they look quite at peace with the world and themselves. It's almost a harking back to the carefree days of old.

This evening, they have no sub goalkeeper. Glen Kelly has been struggling with sickness for two weeks and is out of action after intense speculation he would start today's game. The regular reserve Stephen Enright is still recovering from a broken leg. And so the veteran Andy Hubbard, who only came back to bolster the squad last month, is handed the number 16 shirt. And he's thrown the number 23 shirt for good measure. He will act as cover for Tom Wall but will also sit on the bench to cover for the forwards.

He has little experience between the sticks but seems unfazed.

'No point in worrying about it now,' he laughs. 'Let's just hope Tom stays on his feet.'

And so Waterford have arrived with only six subs – and are quickly reduced to five when Cillian O'Keeffe clashes heads with Maurice O'Gorman in the warm-up and gets stitches before the game has even started. Clearly shaken, and whiter than white, he's effectively ruled out before the ball is even thrown in.

Talk is of limited value now. Kiely asks the team for one last massive effort and then throws his usual shimmy by calling on Dave Kenneally, the stamina trainer, to say a few words. The lads listen because Kenneally has walked the walk with them; he's been there on many dark, shitty nights these past three years. They respect him.

After Kenneally's *cúpla focal* it's out into the evening sunshine. They receive a warm ovation from the locals. There's a growing awareness of the work Kiely and company are doing and people respect their efforts.

Drawing Meath in the qualifiers was cruel luck, and the visitors are hoping for some relief in terms of the coin toss; getting the strong wind at their backs for the first half would at least give them a chance to settle. They don't even get that, of course. Meath will start with the breeze.

'Jesus, we can't even win a toss,' Tom Condon sighs as he makes his way down the sideline with an armful of cones and tracksuit tops.

Going Down Fighting

The soft embrace of the home crowd turns into a friendly shoulder within just five minutes. And that's a good thing. Waterford are all over Meath; they own the ball and are throwing it around the park like Harlem Globetrotters. Meath can't lay a hand on it. Wayne Hennessy and Patrick Hurney are on fire and score quick points. But true to type, Waterford spurn two goal chances. The end product just isn't there.

To add to the frustration, Ger Power, their chief goal-scoring threat, limps off after only six minutes. With most of the game still to go, there are only four fit subs left.

After 15 minutes the minnows still lead by a point and the natives are getting restless. The home fans stand up and roar abuse at their manager, Eamon O'Brien, and his players. They need hardly worry. The fact is Waterford are not growing in stature. They're playing good football but have retreated too far; the waves of green and gold are starting to roll over them.

Eventually the pressure tells. With acres of space around him the Meath corner-back Chris O'Connor posts two quick points and the floodgates soon open.

Thomas O'Gorman hasn't given Cian Ward, the Meath dangerman, a sniff of the action, but the likes of Joe Sheridan, Brian Farrell and Cormac

McGuinness are making hay. And though the Waterford full-back line – the O'Gormans and Shane Briggs – are imperious, serious gaps are opening up elsewhere.

Some of the visitors are bursting blood vessels but others seem to be hiding. Meath take advantage and from long range hit point after point. By half-time it's 0-12 to 0-3. Game over.

In the Waterford dressing room, anger and frustration are rife. As the lads gather their thoughts they let each other have it. It doesn't get personal but they are pissed off at how they've retreated after such a bright opening to the game.

'Not even a bit of fucking pride in the jersey,' shouts Briggs at no one in particular.

One remarkable feature of the Waterford season has been that, amid all the ups and downs, tensions rarely spiral out of control. The players are big enough to criticise and take flak but they've been together too long and respect each other too much to ever get personal.

But for the first time this year, even the management recognise this as a lost cause. Sensing the ship is sunk they merely plead for a bit of pride and point out that a few scores will get Meath thinking again. Paul McLoughlin asks for a performance to leave them heartened. Kiely tells them to go out and throw the kitchen sink for the next 35 minutes.

Which in fairness they do. They hit four of five points straight away, brilliant scores from Hennessy, Hurney and Tony Grey, who marks himself out as a top-class player with his sprints from deep. He also crashes the ball off the crossbar as Waterford miss their third clear goal chance of the game. Liam Ó Líonáin adds two points.

But Meath come back, hitting another string of points and then, in the dying seconds, twist the bayonet by ghosting in for the game's only goal. It ends 1-20 to 0-8.

Waterford's season may be over. But at least they've gone down fighting and with a bit of pride in their hearts.

Jackson's Way

Jackson grabs the microphone at the top of the bus and thanks the squad for their efforts.

'You all know what I think of you,' he says. 'You put in a massive effort and I couldn't ask any more.'

He's a wee bit emotional so he keeps it shorter than usual. For five years now he's been raging against the odds, trying to keep the flag flying. He was not flawless, but then he was not aiming for perfection – his brief was to get them competitive. He's managed that.

The players appreciate what he's invested in the set-up and they don't need a grand speech to remind them. They applaud his few words and he sits down.

Jackson has spent the past 14 years working with the county junior and senior teams and in that time he has received not a euro in expenses. He wouldn't take one if he was offered. There was one Christmas when a gift voucher arrived in the post after they had won the All-Ireland junior title – and he thought long and hard about accepting even that.

In an era when managers and mercenary trainers are pulling down €30,000 a year and more for their troubles, John Kiely is the ultimate volunteer. Officially, he's entitled to claim mileage for going to training and travelling to matches but the county board know they'll be waiting a while for his invoice. Other cash-strapped county boards must look on in envy.

'There's money out there and it's going to managers but I'm not sure it's coming from the county boards,' Kiely points out. 'In most cases wealthy business people or supporters have stepped forward and handed over a few bob to get a big-name manager in or whatever. But I'm doing what I love. Why would you take money for doing something you love in an amateur sport? That's not what the GAA is about.'

In his eyes it's about the volunteer and the love of the game.

'It's about those lads. They deserve all the credit for injecting a bit of pride into Waterford football,' he says, jabbing a finger toward the team.

'Take someone like Tony Grey. He wasn't really in my plans at the start of the year – he was injured. After a few weeks he got right but couldn't get a game. He came to me one evening and said it straight out: "What the fuck do I have to do to get into the team?" I respect that. I told him he would get his chance and, do you know what, he has really taken it.

'As for the O'Gormans – well, if they were playing with Kerry or Tyrone they would be All-Stars. They'd have big deals with Puma and Adidas and the media would be writing about them all the time.

'My heart has gone out to other warriors like Paul Ogle, Mick Ahearne and Gary Hurney. I'm pure devastated at the way things have turned out for them this season.

'And do you know what? We got no luck this year. Cork and Meath in the championship. Jesus, any team that would beat them would be looking at an All-Ireland title.

'But I look around and see Antrim in an Ulster final, Wicklow and Sligo in round three of the qualifiers and Clare only beaten by a few points by Donegal in Ballybofey. We've taken on all those teams in Division 4 and stood our ground. Last year we won five league games. This year we won four and two in the McGrath Cup. We're doing the best we can.'

Not that everyone notices.

'No, some people don't want to notice,' he says. 'I read an article lately by Joe Brolly. I had never read or heard from Joe that he had been involved with the Antrim footballers until they reached the Ulster final. But then I heard him harping on about it quite a lot.

'Joe started writing about how pleased he was for those Antrim players to be so successful this season, having seen them lose out on promotion in 2008 to a Waterford side that resembled a pub team. To be called a pub team after the work we've put in, well that's a disgrace – in fact it's one of the worst insults that was ever directed at us. It made my blood boil.

'But sure that's what we put up with. As I said, there was no word of Joe and Antrim until the boys reached an Ulster final and they were in the big time all of a sudden. Then it suited Joe to come out with all this stuff.'

He can only try to change perceptions. But if he had his way there are other things about the game Kiely would change. He'd get rid of the league for a start and would expand the championship.

'I'd have four groups of eight teams that would play six games each,' he says. 'Put the top 16 in a battle for the Sam Maguire and the bottom 16 in another championship. That way guys get games during the summer.

'I'd be looking for the local fixtures to be streamlined a bit better, but Timmy O'Keeffe is an honest man, a straight talker, and he will sort that out.'

Whether Kiely will be around to benefit from the new county secretary's good work remains to be seen. In mid-autumn 2009 the football board will meet to make a call. They have a choice – keep Kiely or replace him with a new man.

After five years Jackson has brought the team to a different level. If he's jettisoned he won't take another job outside Waterford. The chances are that the county board will opt for a new voice, a new man to 'freshen things up' and try new things. If they do he won't cause a fuss.

'I won't be bitter if I don't get it next year,' he says. 'I'll wish the new man the best of luck and will contact the boys to thank them for all their help.'

If he does get back in he'll make several more changes. The laissez-faire approach to weights training will go and he'll insist on every player doing weekly core exercises. If he could unearth a couple more forwards, the likes of Brian O'Halloran, he'd be inclined to play a normal six-two-six formation instead of having to drag so many bodies behind the ball.

'We had no other choice but to employ that tactic,' he says. 'Sure we were leaking six goals a game before we came in. But in order to go back to a more traditional line-up I'd need Gary Hurney as a target man.'

He's a firm believer in the ethos of the club but would still like exclusive access to players for two weeks before championship matches.

'The club has to survive,' he acknowledges. 'We all go back there at some stage. But for big championship matches, a county team needs first call on players – just for two weeks beforehand. That should be achievable.

'Look, whether I get back or not, I've done my bit. There were a few guys who maybe wanted a new voice last year so maybe they'll get their way now. I just know how much I've enjoyed it, the loyalty of my players and backroom team.

'I never fell out with anyone on the board and I see the Waterford footballers as real Corinthians – defending the spirit of the county against all the odds. And doing it for no real rewards. Forget London and the other disappointments; it was a privilege to serve with them.'

His fate will be decided at a board meeting in September 2009. Already, there are rumblings a new man will be installed.

'We'll wait and see how it goes,' he says. 'If I get it we'll lift it up a notch again. If I don't I'll be involved in the game in some shape or form anyway, although I would never go outside the county. No matter who is in charge, I just hope Waterford football gets what it deserves.'

Being denied successive promotions means there might be something missing from his managerial CV but it's unlikely Waterford football will ever again have such a tireless servant. After all he's achieved it's little wonder he's happy in his own skin.

No matter how you dress it up, his appointment as junior manager 10 years ago and senior manager five years later were seismic moments.

For him this job was always about emotional ties.

And they will never be cut.

*   *   *

Meanwhile, the football board prepare to make a call on Jackson and his backroom team. They have phoned around, canvassed opinions here and there and sought the views of the senior players.

For a penetrating analysis they should have asked Stephen Cunningham. There will be no more threshing in the field for this guy but he's definitely management material for the future. Even when the team was being pummelled in the dark old days, his on-pitch demeanour was a loud rebuttal of the dire straits in which they often found themselves.

Now that he has found harbour, he's at peace with the world. As he sits down to rewind the years there is no recrimination, no hint of sourness. He prefers to focus on the Kiely era, when, given a transfusion of new blood as it were, they stood up and fought their corner.

'When the hidings and the hammerings died down and Jackson came in, I got serious satisfaction playing to the highest level I could,' he recalls. 'I learned from better players and I think I did as well as I could.

'It was set in stone that this would be my last year. I've had too many injuries and it was only against Tipp and Wexford that I was coming right. I did my ankle against Wexford and was at nothing against Meath.'

During his career he learned every trick in the book, majoring in how to keep opponents at bay, stalling on the ball, switching play crossfield, giving his marker the odd little trip or block, anything to keep his team in the game. But he never slackened.

From the first to the final whistle.

'Look, I remember playing Cavan in 2005 and they put seven goals past us before half-time. My brother Eoin was in goal and the funny thing was he pulled off several tremendous saves. So you never really get away from that negative attitude of trying to keep the score down.

'But near the end of my time we went out to win most games we played and, if we lost a league game it would only be by a couple of points, compared to 10 or 20 a few years back. So we've been pretty competitive and that's all I ever wanted. Success would have been nice, but it wasn't to be.'

Retiring will leave a void in his life; the intercounty project dictated his every waking hour.

'Sure I'll miss it, no point in saying otherwise. I took great pride in playing and it kept me in great shape. It would be with me at breakfast; you might feel like a fry but you'd have cereal. It would be with you in the evenings when you might fancy a bit of chocolate but you'd go training instead. On your nights off there were times when you could either curl up on the couch or go stretching. I'd go stretching.

'When my friends would be out having a few pints, you'd be in looking forward to playing against some of the best Gaelic footballers in the country. That was my buzz. That was my life. But sure I'll have to throw myself into this house we're building now. That will be my new project.'

Nowadays in Irish sport, there is way too much weight placed on winning, too much commotion over those who land trophies and not enough respect shown to those who battle against the tide, trying to keep the ship afloat. Cunningham never got to tread the boards in the championship's great summer theatres but he played his part all the same, understated though it was.

'The one and only thing that does upset me slightly is that I've looked on and seen the likes of Limerick, Wexford, Tipperary and Fermanagh all go on these amazing runs, winning league titles and reaching All-Ireland semi-finals. Why didn't we achieve something like that?

'I would be a little envious of those teams, but only because I feel we were as good as them. We beat Wexford and Tipp several times in the league. There was never anything between us and Limerick, and I just wonder why we didn't get a hop. But then I look at our draw this year. Cork and Meath. Sure you wouldn't have a hope.'

Putting certain bad days behind him – like the one in Ruislip – will be a relief. That cross-channel disaster was the starkest illustration of how Waterford have repeatedly tortured themselves these past few years, just when it looked like release from their house of pain was imminent.

Now is the time to consign those memories to the inner chambers of his mind and turn the key from the outside. The new house and job will keep him occupied. In the past, he reneged on career opportunities in order to give football his undivided attention.

It's time to change the focus.

'I'd like to drive up the ladder in the accountancy business,' he says. 'I'll devote myself to going as far as I can. I have to think outside of football now. Jesus, I never imagined I'd hear myself saying those words.'

One last time he sifts through a medley of memories. All the things that remind him of why he devoted a third of his life to the jersey. Days when they dined at the top table as guests of the likes of Cork, Kerry and Meath. The lads. Jackson. The challenge. Defying the odds. Being the best he could be. They were the best of times.

Cunningham was one of the stalwarts who kept the Waterford wagon train on the road to greener pastures. When the pace faltered or they lost direction, he steadied them as best he could. But he has stepped off the trail and pitched his tent for good now.

Time to let someone else work on the dream.

July 17, Chicago, USA

THE sun is dipping low behind Sears Tower as Mick Ahearne, the half-forgotten man of Waterford football, checks out the view from the skydeck of Chicago's tallest skyscraper.

His mind is brimming with thoughts. Football, health, the future. Last week he hit New York to recharge the batteries, and after a few days in Manhattan he caught a flight to the Windy City. He's enjoying the break away from schoolteaching and away from football.

He's a long time on the road with Waterford, and this season – like most other Waterford seasons – finished with a wobble. His own direct involvement ended out West. Clearly struggling against Sligo, he was replaced at a time when the points were still up for grabs and promotion was still possible. He'd never before felt the shepherd's hook in the championship, and it hurt badly.

Something wasn't right. The natural strength seemed to be draining from his limbs. Exercise was proving painful. He went for tests, but they proved inconclusive; one prognosis offered was that a virus had found its way into his bloodstream. Looking all of a stone lighter now, he's still trying to identify the ailment. There's a bit of power back in the legs and he's managed a few club games.

'I don't even know if it's fully gone yet,' he says of the mystery illness. 'Please God it is. I've been able to tip away with Kill so it can't be too bad. Was I worried? Yeah, I was. The doctors tested me for everything under the sun and of course you fear the worst. But all the results came back clear and I had a bit more relief.'

Since the illness he's ploughed his own furrow. He travelled to Navan under his own steam to watch the team's swansong. It didn't leave him rocking in the aisles.

'I was actually disgusted with what I saw,' he admits. 'We didn't even put up a fight. After 20 minutes they walked right through us. I looked out on the field and saw some lads breaking their balls but others hiding.

'It's the same way in training – some lads go flat out and others come in late and take shortcuts. Sure you'd wonder about going back into that.'

Despite the frustration at the team's failure and his own stunted season, you get the feeling Ahearne will return to camp once his body permits. It's clear he still cares passionately. And when you care that much about something it invariably brings you back to the starting post.

He simply has too much to offer not to go again and the team needs him now more than ever.

Likewise Paul Ogle, who underwent surgery on 18 August. Major surprise – he's already bulling for road.

'I can't wait to get back again. A lot will have to change in the set-up but I'm still hopeful we can climb the ladder. We played great football in patches this season. And look what the other Division 4 teams have done this year.'

His teammates go their different ways and weigh up next season's possibilities. Ger Power also tore his other cruciate and now faces a year

216

on the sidelines. Eddie Rockett transferred from Portlaw to Stradbally in a bid to play serious football and win a county title.

The flying half-back Tony Grey – now a clubmate of Ogle's at Stradbally – also picked up an injury and didn't lace a boot for weeks after the Meath game.

Liam Lawlor, Patrick Hurney and Brian Wall went on to play on the Waterford intermediate hurling team that lost a Munster final to Cork.

Shane Walsh was sprung from the bench for the county senior hurlers and scored the winning goal in their epic All-Ireland quarter-final comeback against Galway. He repeated the trick twice against Kilkenny in the All-Ireland semi-final with a smashing brace of goals but saw his team fail narrowly to make the final, as Gary Hurney looked on from the sideline with a broken collarbone.

Seán O'Hare was on the county U-21 squad that lost to Clare in the Munster final but has a bright future ahead. Meanwhile, it's curtains for the recalled veteran Andy Hubbard who retired again, most likely fearful he'd become the regular sub-keeper.

The O'Gormans, Power, O'Keeffe, Hennessy, Wall, Briggs and Ó Líonáin went back to their clubs to fulfil domestic hurling and football duties.

As these guys reflect on the 2009 season, some solace could surely be taken in the fact that their two championship conquerors, Cork and Meath, reached an All-Ireland final and All-Ireland semi-final respectively. Their Division 4 colleagues Antrim made the Ulster final, Wicklow went on an amazing run in the qualifiers, while Sligo pushed Galway all the way in the Connacht semi-final.

But they've spent long enough looking at other teams taking off on marvellous odysseys. It's high time they seized the opportunity themselves.

Epilogue

Standing in the freezing cold of Fraher Field on the first Sunday in January watching Waterford play in the McGrath Cup, I wondered if I'd finally lost the plot.

Back home in Nenagh, the fire was lit and holiday season TV was calling but instead there I was fighting hypothermia and taking in a game that the outside world didn't give two hoots about.

There were many other occasions during the season when I questioned my sanity. Flying to London to watch the lads lose to the home side was just one of them. But I stayed with it.

The reason? My job as a GAA writer had taken a turn and the games and personalities were starting to become secondary. I found myself covering player strikes, interviewing industrial relations executives, quizzing Department of Arts, Sport and Tourism officials over grants. I think everyone involved in Gaelic games needed a reality check. I definitely needed something different anyway.

So I rang John Kiely.

We met 10 years earlier and we clicked. Soon after he was appointed senior football manager of Waterford, I popped down to him to take in a training session, wrote a feature on my experience for the *Sunday Independent* and I couldn't get that visit out of my head.

I was struck by his players' energy, their boundless enthusiasm for what seemed like a lost cause. In October 2008, I asked John for permission to join the team for the 2009 season. He said it would be no problem.

I started my research, made tabs on the relevant personnel and by the end of the campaign, I was part of the furniture. I travelled all over Ireland with them, hit every league and championship game, took in each challenge match, attended their training sessions and drove to Dungarvan for team meetings.

When people asked if I was off my head I really didn't have much of a defence. Deep down, though, I was delighted. I was seeking to soak up a story of grassroots GAA at its most vulnerable and most wholesome and when I met people like John, Mick O'Loughlin, Paul Ogle and Mick Ahearne I knew I was on the right track.

They sucked me right in.

I spent the spring dissecting the Division 4 league table, trying to predict the outcomes of upcoming fixtures, almost willing Waterford to promotion. I won't tell you a lie; I made a few bob along the way too. There was such general apathy out there towards this team, such a lack of respect from the public and the bookies that it was pretty easy to make a handicap bet and win €100 here and there. In the first NFL match against Wicklow, for instance, the bookies had Waterford at even money to lose by eight points. They were way off; the lads drew away from home. That result, at least, paid for the diesel for my journey to Aughrim.

Waterford's season ended with a loss to Meath in Navan and about an hour after the final whistle I trooped silently out of the dressing room, disconsolate that my journey was finally over. There was a nice touch just as I made my exit – John Phelan spotted me slipping away and quietly insisted that I receive a jersey before I left. Class. That shirt means more to me than they could imagine.

At the start of the year I felt awkward hanging around the dressing room. Even though I'd spent most of my youth in dressing rooms, I was acutely aware as a journalist that it was a private place, a safe haven for the lads where they could lay themselves bare. The first few outings saw me clumsily traipse inside just as the keynote speeches were about to be delivered. But no one ever objected to my presence. Kiely told them I was dovetailing them for the year and to get used to it.

I tried to stay as inconspicuous as possible, head down, mouth shut but as the league unfolded I was made to feel so comfortable that I began breezing about the place like I held their franchise, joining the subs on the bench or shooting the breeze with the backroom boys.

When Jackson asked me for my tuppenceworth before the match against Sligo he only did so because he could see the passion in my eyes. By then they all knew I cared, that I wasn't there to take the mickey out of them and so they completely opened up.

Not once did a player turn me down for an interview or chat. In fact, they couldn't really understand why anyone would be interested in them. They spoke openly of their hopes and their ups and downs in life. After every conversation, my admiration for those lads grew a little more. Meanwhile, back in my day job, I grew to have even less tolerance for players from bigger counties who were whinging about issues and luxurious extras that the Waterford lads would never even dream of drawing down.

They won six games all year, probably more than a Waterford football team has ever managed and my only regret is that they didn't make it out of Division 4. This was their big chance, no doubt about it. That leap will be all the harder now with big guns like Limerick and Longford relegated to that bottom tier. The team's task is only harder.

And they'll have to do it without Jackson.

On 12 September 2009, it emerged that his term as manager was up. The football board convened a couple of times and decided not to renew his term. Five years, they reckoned, was enough and so they appointed Johnny Owens, the former Tipperary star player and manager, to the role. What a task the new man has on his hands – the bottom division is now more competitive than ever.

Jackson wasn't even asked if he wanted to stay on so it was clear from a long way out that change was the order of the day. Once the season ended that was it.

When I spoke to the backroom guys they were very upset, disgusted even, that John hadn't been contacted to find out if he was interested in another year. In their final text to the squad, one of the backroom stated that 'it was a disgrace that a true Waterford Gael had been treated in such fashion'. In fairness to the players they immediately contacted him and rallied around as the news broke.

Soon after, I sought reaction from Jackson and he was pretty down about the way things had been handled, but his first instinct was to wish the new man all the best.

'I wish John Owens every success and the players too,' he said. 'It will be a tough job but I will be there supporting them all the way. When we took over five years ago the flame was nearly extinct, we lit that torch again and kept it burning. We narrowly missed promotion twice so obviously the board are bringing the new man in to get that promotion. That has to be his mandate. And I will be the happiest man in Waterford if that's achieved.

'As regards my own feelings, what's the point in being bitter? This is the GAA and the GAA is my life, good, bad and ugly. I won't be dragged down to the level of making outlandish statements. I love the thing and met some decent people in my time in charge. I had some lovely, honest lads who played for me and they have been in contact ever since the news broke. We turned a lot of them from unknown quantities into decent intercounty footballers. In the course of my time we got seven Waterford men onto the Munster team to play in the Railway Cup. All over Ireland I met friends through this job. Most importantly, I suppose, I had the complete loyalty of my backroom team.

'Looking back, I think we won more games in the last 2 years than Waterford did in the previous 30. So I am very disappointed by this news. I am going to miss the job.

'After five years in charge I wasn't even asked about staying on and that's the most disappointing thing but we get on with it. It's all about the friends I made in the GAA family, not about the people making decisions behind your back. I certainly won't be going around sulking, that's not my style. If I do that, I'm only letting myself down.'

Had the team not blown it against London, the season would surely have enjoyed a grand finale. Everyone involved knows that. Waterford would more than likely have made Division 3 and Jackson would most likely have remained at the helm. But it didn't happen and though some of the players expressed their guilt that it never happened, Jackson instead prefers to credit them for how they fought to rectify the cross-channel collapse.

From the outside, the new manager will have to seek more cooperation from clubs and the county board in terms of fixtures if he is to finally make the leap to Division 3. John Owens now gets the chance to put his stamp on Waterford football.

'The delegates just felt that change was needed,' explained Tom Cunningham, chairman of the football board and county board vice-chairman. 'John was terrific, he gave an unreal commitment and rose the standards, he brought great honour to Waterford football but there was a mood for change and that's why John Owens was ratified,' he added.

It remains to be seen how the new regime can transform things. One thing's for sure – it would be nice if a few spectators turned out to lend them a bit of moral support.

One conversation I had with Paul McLoughlin during the year really struck a chord with me. He was referring to an element of the set-up that he just couldn't get his head around.

'Waterford is supposed to be a sports-mad county,' he said, 'that's what they pride themselves on. But we never see anyone at our games, home or away. I would estimate that we have six or seven real supporters. The rest don't give a shit. We're bloody lepers. I can't get my head around the fact that locals prefer to stay at home in front of the telly and watch Doncaster play Plymouth Argyle on a Sunday rather than come and lend us a hand. But that's what's happening and it sickens me.'

He is spot on. It really is this team against the rest. Maybe that explains why, despite all the frustrations, injuries, the loss to London and the other ups and downs, there wasn't one serious outburst or row among the squad all year long. My only reasoning for this is that the lads know they're all in it together. There's just no point in turning on each other.

Jackson liked to keep his panel compact and it worked to the extent that there was little bickering or bitching, but a lot of new players will have to be blooded now. There were only 18 fit players available for their final game of the 2009 season, but with Cunningham retired, Ogle, Ahearne and Power struggling with injuries and the dual players unlikely to play any role at all in the 2010 season, new blood is vital to keep the show ticking over.

As I look back on the year, I have to say I gained a useful perspective on the complexities involved in keeping a team going at this level.

There was a very relaxed approach to the set-up and maybe at times it was too laid-back; a lot of players said as much during the year. On the other hand, though, you simply won't get players to line out at this level if you decide to run a military regime. There almost *has* to be some element of light-heartedness involved to get them out in force and keep them interested. If you play the heavy hand in Division 4, it's even harder to entice and maintain the best footballers with so many other attractions around.

On the field, their fitness and stamina levels were superb and their link-up play and passing was often out of the top drawer but their attitude to weights training and shooting in front of the posts was pretty poor. I couldn't understand how the forwards insisted, time and again, on running the ball into the 14-yard-line before contemplating a shot. So many times they were bottled up or ran into cul-de-sacs. There was a huge reluctance to shoot from distance or anywhere outside the 21-yard-line. It cost them dearly.

They also lack a natural attacker, a guy to clip three or four points over the bar every game. If they had one, they would have made it up to Division 3 this season. Against London, when they shot wide after wide, that glaring deficiency was never as obvious. Liam Ó Líonáin may be a goal machine but he's better deployed running against defences – the team is crying out for an inside-forward with a bit of poise. Young Brian O'Halloran would solve that problem but he's on the Waterford minor hurling team and is a star there too. He'll face the familiar tug of war in the next two years and no prizes for guessing which way he'll turn.

With so many of the team involved in club hurling and football, the majority of players couldn't even spare a night to pump weights and it showed as the campaign unfolded – they were knocked off the ball way too easily at times. It goes without saying that if they want to progress, they quickly need to address that.

Tactically, they were hard to break down. Up until the championship started they only conceded an average of nine points per game. Cork, their Munster conquerors, went on to contest an All-Ireland final, while Meath reached the semi-final – demonstrating how tough Waterford's draw was. Luck was most definitely not on their side when the balls with the team names were being plucked out of the hat.

But luck alone won't do it for you. If the lads are ever going to progress, they need to take control over the club v county dilemma. I noticed that clubs sometimes insisted on taking the footballers away just for hurling challenge matches. Only the players themselves can solve that issue. They will continue to be dragged here and there until they shout stop. For as long as that drags on, the footballers will have no proper preparation for the championship. Every year they run a tight ship for the league but it all goes pear-shaped once summer comes and the domestic hurling campaign looms. Unless the players lay down the law to their clubs, I can't see things changing.

They possess many strengths. Absolute unity, stability of personnel and a pretty watertight defence. By now, you will have grasped their weaknesses. Their past weighs them down like an anchor; they've been down in the depths for so long that they shrink when opportunity knocks. Hesitancy in front of the posts has dogged them as has not being able to consistently field their best players.

Still, I'll forever remember with fondness my season on the sidelines with these men.

To witness at first hand 20 to 25 lads laying themselves bare and doing all they can to keep the team going forward against the odds is a humbling experience. I was privileged to be part of it.

I really hope this book demonstrated how wide the gap is between top and bottom. There's such a gulf, it's ridiculous.

My final wish is that this book might give all of us GAA folk a bit of perspective on things. The next time a team decides to down tools or kick up a stink about some controversy or other they would do well to think of the Waterford lads and their ongoing struggle to make a modest dream come true.

Sure, it's great to have the big stars and packed houses in September, but let's not forget about the underdog either.

Teams like the Waterford footballers are the real heroes.

I know that now.

Tunnel Vision

Behind the Scenes at Great Irish Sports Events

Tadhg de Brún

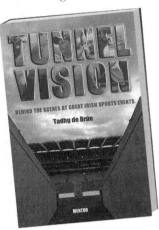

Tunnel Vision takes the reader where no Irish sports book has ever gone before – behind the scenes at great Irish sporting events – from the Irish Open to the Heineken Cup to the All-Ireland Finals. Over 30 years with RTÉ Sports as event/floor manager has given Tadhg de Brún a unique insight into the stories and secrets at all the biggest Irish sporting events.

- Memories of the Irish Open – the golfers, their egos and their problems – and some very rewarding bets placed by the RTÉ crew!
- Snooker Finals at Goffs – the tension and the chaos; how Dennis Taylor was neatly put in his 'seat' after complaining about the facilities.
- All-Ireland Final days – the craziness *not* shown on TV; how the Kilkenny captain emerged from the victorious dressing room dressed in boots and gear and rushed off to church.
- The characters you meet on the road – the managers, players, caterers, cleaners, as well as the rakes of Liberty Square and the security man at the Brandywell. The comedy and tragedy of their lives as witnessed on great sporting occasions.
- Behind the great events of the Charlton Era, including an eventful trip by Tadhg and his crew to the World Cup in America in 1994.

Bainisteoir

The 10 Greatest GAA Managers

Finbarr McCarthy

Bainisteoir tells the individual heroic stories of the GAA's 10 most successful managers – based on personal interviews given to the author.

- **Dublin's** Kevin Heffernan – how he trained the Dubs' teams for victory.
- **Kerry's** Mick O'Dwyer – the secrets of his long run of success with the Kingdom – and **Kildare**, **Laois** and **Wicklow**.
- **Kilkenny's** Brian Cody –the 4-in-a-row, his research, 'player management' and training routines.
- **Cork's** Billy Morgan – dogged by controversy and his outspoken nature – yet **he** achieved great things down South.
- **Meath's** Seán Boylan – how he combined an outstanding run of success with the 'royal' county and his role of 'Healer'.
- **Clare's** Ger Loughnane – followed by controversy at both Clare and **Galway** but he's a great motivator and retains the will to win.
- **Tyrone's** Mickey Harte – outsmarted Kerry and motivated his players to success.
- **Kerry's** Páidí Ó Sé – straight-talking stewardship of the Kingdom, and later with **Westmeath** and then . . . **Clare**.
- **Cork's** Jimmy Barry Murphy – hurling success on Leeside with an Adidas controversy and Greyhound-racing hobby.
- **Armagh's** Joe Kernan – how he achieved three-in-a-row in the Ulster Championship.

Larry Cunningham

A Showband Legend

Tom Gilmore

Despite a number of heart attacks, a cancer scare and several attempts at retirement, showband legend Larry Cunningham is still singing in his 70s. His story is a *potpourri* of humour, success, shady deals – as well as sadness, death and murder on the music scene.

Larry Cunningham was the first Irish artist to make the UK Pop Charts – long before U2, the Boomtown Rats, Boyzone or Westlife. His 'Tribute to Jim Reeves' spent over three months in the British hit parade, sold more than a quarter of a million copies and culminated in his appearance on *Top of the Pops* alongside Cliff Richard and others.

When 'Gentleman Jim' Reeves walked off the stage at a dance in Donegal, Larry's singing of Reeves' songs stopped an angry mob from burning the place down. His first No. 1 'Lovely Leitrim' sold over a quarter of a million but the song has sad links to a bloody shooting in a New York bar. The gunfight and deaths, as well as two forgotten song verses, are recalled in this book.

Fascinating reading for those interested in Showbands and Sixties nostalgia, Country 'n' Irish music, the rise and decline of the Ballroom dances and Jimmy Magee GAA All-Stars Football charity.

The Dark Side of Celebrity

Irish Courtroom Scandals of the Rich and Famous
LIAM COLLINS

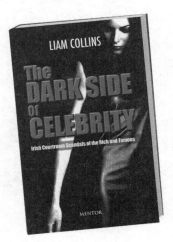

A journey to the other side of fame – telling the story of Ireland's rich and famous fighting each other across the courtroom floor. The stories of the sexual affairs, the alcohol abuse, the dirty tricks and the greed that ruined relationships and tore friendships apart.

- The beauty queen Michelle Rocca's bitter courtroom battle with Ryanair heir Cathal Ryan over a brawl at a socialite's birthday party.
- Solicitor-to-the-stars Elio Malocco and his dodgy dealings – leading to a falling out with Twink, the de Valera familly and the entire Law Society!
- How Manchester United boss Sir Alex Ferguson fell out with his Irish friend John Magnier over the wonder horse Rock of Gibraltar.
- How the sex of Bono's baby became a central issue in a court case that had absolutely nothing to do with him or U2.
- The Illusionist Paul Goldin disappears from a theatre stage and turns up in Hawaii with 'the other woman'.

Irish Family Feuds

Battles over Money, Sex and Power

LIAM COLLINS

When families fall out, the bitterness that emerges is matched only by the ferocity of their attacks on each other. Family feuds are far more vicious than disputes between strangers, as family members compete to crush each other completely and without mercy.

Cases include many rich and famous Irish families:
- Ben v Margaret – Duel at Dunnes
- The PV Doyle family 'hotel' war
- Comans and the 'Pub brawl'
- Enya, Clannad and the Brennan family feud
- 'Volkswagon vendetta' – the O'Flahertys' family secret

and many more family feuds over money, power and sex.

Irish Crimes of Passion

Killing for Love, Lust and Desire

LIAM COLLINS

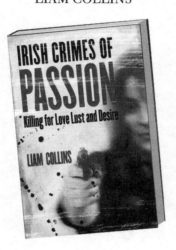

Liam Collins investigates the tragic cases where love, lust, desire and jealousy twist and contort in a spiral of madness.

- Picture the beautiful temptress who buys her own grave, then lures her lover to a dramatic death scene in her bedroom . . .
- the husband who goes through his wife's mobile phone messages and unleashes a rage that not only leads to her murder but wipes out an entire family . . .
- or the coward brooding in a love triangle who hires a ruthless killer to murder his pregnant wife.

They are all here in the hidden Ireland, where ordinary men and women suddenly get caught up in that deadly moment when crime and passion collide.